Backstage Pass

True Stories from Corvallis, Oregon

Published in Beaverton, Oregon, by Good Catch Publishing.
www.goodcatchpublishing.com
V1.1

Printed in the United States of America

Table of Contents

Acknowledgements

I would like to thank Steve Minton for his vision for this book and Karen Bell for her hard work in making it a reality. To the people of Kings Circle, thank you for your boldness and vulnerability in sharing your personal stories.

This book would not have been published without the amazing efforts of our project manager and editor, Samantha Jaquez. Her untiring resolve pushed this project forward and turned it into a stunning victory. Thank you for your great fortitude and diligence. Deep thanks to our incredible editor in chief, Michelle Cuthrell, and executive editor, Jen Genovesi, for all the amazing work they do. I would also like to thank our invaluable proofreader, Melody Davis, for the focus and energy she puts into perfecting our words.

Lastly, I want to extend our gratitude to the creative and very talented Ariana Randle, who designed the beautiful cover for *Backstage Pass: True Stories from Corvallis, Oregon.*

Daren Lindley
President and CEO
Good Catch Publishing

The book you are about to read
is a compilation of authentic life stories.
The facts are true, and the events are real.
These storytellers have dealt with crisis, tragedy, abuse
and neglect and have shared their most private moments,
mess-ups and hang-ups in order for others to learn and
grow from them. In order to protect the identities of those
involved in their pasts, the names and details of some
storytellers have been withheld or changed.

Introduction

What do you do when life careens out of control? When addiction overtakes you or abuse chains you with fear? Is depression escapable? Will relationships ever be healthy again? Are you destined to dissolve into an abyss of sorrow? Or will the sunlight of happiness ever return?

Your life really can change. It is possible to become a new person. The seven stories you are about to read prove positively that people right here in our town have stopped dying and started living. Whether you've been beaten by abuse, broken promises, shattered dreams or suffocating addictions, the resounding answer is, "Yes! You can become a new person." The potential to break free from gloom and into a bright future awaits.

Expect inspiration, hope and transformation! As you walk with these real people from our very own city through the pages of this book, you will not only find riveting accounts of their hardships, you will learn the secrets that brought about their breakthroughs. These people are no longer living in the shadows of yesterday; they are thriving with a sense of mission and purpose *today*. We hope these stories inspire you to do the same.

Great Love
The Story of Eric
Written by Audrey Jackson

People die in their own vomit.

My face brushed against the carpet, surrounded by a huge puddle of Dijon yellow liquid. The smell was putrid — a mixture of peppermint Schnapps, tequila and chocolate syrup. Chunks of food, eaten gluttonously the night before, floated in the puddle, which had begun to seep into the fibers of the short shag carpet. The light from the window blinded me, and it made my temples pulse like a drum line practice in my head. I reached around and felt the back of my T-shirt. It was wet with vomit and sweat. Rolling onto my back, I stared out into the distance. The panes of my apartment's windows framed a mid-afternoon sun, so bright it almost lacked color. My head continued to pulse as the smell of my insides, plastered onto my cotton shirt, reached my nostrils.

Is this who I want to be? Is this the life I want to live?

❧❧❧

Mom was 17 when she got pregnant with me. She was a senior in high school and was taken advantage of by a guy at a party one night. Date rape, I guess you could call it. The doctors told her that statistically she wouldn't be able to do it — raise a kid and finish high school. But she was adamant about keeping me. I was named after Mom's best friend. He was murdered for the $30 in his wallet and a stereo. And I guess Mom figured she could never bring him back, but she could remember him when she looked at me.

I don't remember us ever struggling. But I guess, looking back, we probably did. Mom was a teenager trying to raise a kid. My first few years, we lived with Mom's parents. Grandma committed suicide when I was 5, though, and Mom's world began turning a lot faster then. We eventually moved out. I can still remember the small one-bedroom apartment we shared with Mom's friend and her son. She had also gotten pregnant senior year of high school, and Tommy had been born a month after me. The two of us didn't know that the way we were being brought up wasn't really normal.

My dad came around to an occasional birthday party. I only know because I used to find old pictures from parties stuck away in Mom's house. I guess he did all that he thought he could. When I turned 18, he handed me a letter telling me that he hoped I would one day be able to understand it all. I'm not sure I ever did.

I was 7 when Steve came along and married my mom. He was a good guy, and I liked him well enough. A year later, my brother Benji was born. And there we were, living in a normal suburban neighborhood in Texas. And while I don't have too many fond memories of our family during those years, we were doing okay for ourselves. Mom and I had somehow beaten the odds.

Great Love

∂∞∂∞∂

I slouched down in the backseat of the white four-door hatchback Volkswagen as Gunner and the other guys from my neighborhood rolled up a joint and passed it back and forth. We were barely 15 — we didn't even have our learner's permits. Gunner had snuck out his second-story window and stolen his mom's car, picking each of us up along the way. I guess Gunner got the idea from his older brother, who'd been known to drive around the neighborhood smoking and drinking rum. He'd also recently left home and moved to California, and in the eyes of us 15-year-old boys, he was a god.

"Let's sneak out tonight," Gunner whispered to us after school that day. And once the moon hung in the sky, we gathered inside his mom's car and took off. Music from a CD mix Gunner created blared out of the side speakers as we made the two-mile loop around the neighborhood.

"Dude, this is killer. Have some more." Brad, sitting in the passenger seat, handed me the bottle of rum. I took another swig. As my head grew lighter, I heard Gunner laughing from the front seat.

"Hand the weed back here, man." Nirvana came through the stereo, and Brad sang along up front.

"Feelin' uninspired ... think I'll start a fire. Everybody runnnnn, Bobby's got a gun."

"Dude, you're a horrible singer."

"Yeah, okay, Mr. Musically Inclined."

I reached up to hand the joint back to Brad right as Gunner hit the accelerator and started speeding down the half-mile of straight neighborhood road. I jerked forward, realizing I had never put on my seatbelt.

"Whoooooooooo!" screamed Brad. "This is it, guys. This is it." He leaned his head out the window and put out his hands. It seemed cool at first, speeding through the dark. We were cutting through the night like bandits in movies we'd seen as kids. The feeling faded, though, when I realized we were drawing close to a sharp curve.

"Gunner, slow down, man." Gunner's foot continued to press down on the accelerator, his eyes lifeless and looking ahead. It was as if he was in a trance. I screamed as we inched closer and closer to the turn.

"Gunner! Wake up, dude. Stop! Slow down!"

"Slow down, man! Are you freaking insane?"

Gunner's head suddenly shook, and his eyes grew large and round. Reaching the curve in the road, he jerked the steering wheel sharply to the left. I flew across the car, slamming into the window's glass. We fishtailed to the left and to the right and then to the left again, almost hitting a red brick mailbox and an old green pickup truck on the side of the road.

Breathless, we sat in silence for a minute or two, listening to the car's GPS speak to us in his mom's native language, French. The smell of burnt rubber filled our nostrils as we quietly and quite mechanically stepped out of the car.

"Dude, what the heck?"

"Gunner, man, what were you thinking? Were you trying to kill us?"

"Shut the heck up."

He walked down the street, arms shaking, and we followed — walking to the sound of our beating hearts and our throbbing heads.

∂∞∂∞∂∞

I can't pinpoint exactly why I started rebelling or why I grew to be so resentful. It started innocently enough, I guess. I started sneaking out of the house late at night to go skateboard with my buddies in the neighborhood around seventh grade. We'd skate for hours and then I'd tiptoe back into the house, usually getting caught by my parents. They'd hold my shoulders and look into my eyes, accusing them of being red.

"Let me see your eyes. Have you been doing drugs?"

"No, I was just out skateboarding." That was always my answer. Until one day it wasn't.

I started smoking weed with the neighborhood boys in about eighth grade. Deep down, I knew it was stupid. I was a smart kid — I made good grades and was in national honor societies, and I guess I had a lot going for me. But deep down, I was angry and confused and didn't want to be the good kid with the good grades. I wanted something or someone to fill the void I felt inside.

So, I ran with the guys I had grown up with. We partied and smoked and cursed till we were sick. But it seemed cool, and at that point, it was all we really cared about. Senior year of high school, Gunner and I formed a band with this guy named Charlie, whose parents had more money than we had ever seen. They lived in this big house that had a cellar with more than a million dollars' worth of wine. One day, Charlie came to band practice and told us his parents were leaving town.

"You guys wanna party tonight?"

"Yeah, man. That sounds cool."

"I have some psychedelic mushrooms we can try, too."

That night, we tried the mushrooms. It opened us up to a whole new world — not a good one. All I remember about the end of that night was that Gunner wandered off into the woods and lay on the ground for several hours, gazing up into the night sky and imagining who knows what.

❧❧❧

Experimenting with different drugs and hallucinogens just became something normal. My friends and I would get together and see how different ones would make us feel. It was more of a hobby than an addiction, at least at that point. The summer before I went to college, I started working at my biological dad's family's restaurant. In business for about 50 years, it was a local favorite. It sat on a corner in what was then not the nicest part of town, and I'd say the outside reflected the type of people my uncle hired to work there. You might say he believed that everyone should have third, fourth and fifth chances to make his or her life right. They were a tough crowd. And I mean actually tough. I worked alongside druggies and alcoholics. They looked like they had seen better days. But it was a job, and I was 19, poor and headed to college.

Mom and I were living alone in a two-bedroom apartment at that point. She and my stepdad had divorced when I started high school. It was the two of us again, though this time I wanted to be anywhere else.

My freshman year of college, I was living at home, working 32 hours a week at the restaurant and attending classes. It was all right, I guess, but there was really no tight-knit community I could cling to. Not many of my friends had chosen to stay in town, and I was working so much I didn't have time for the college life I thought I deserved to have. I wanted to party and live freely and experience all that the world had to offer. But there I was, scrubbing dishes with a bunch of rundown co-workers and going home each night to my mom's apartment.

The desire to experience more and have more fun drove me. And somehow I got wrapped up in pyramid schemes and buying and selling weed and cocaine. It began to be all that I thought about. I'd use the money I'd make at the restaurant to buy weed so that I could not only smoke it, but also go to parties and sell it. I was making bank. It was at one particular party that I started using Ecstasy. The music was loud, and I remember seeing this girl from across the room. The drug made everything look brighter, and I could feel myself getting a rush of blood to my head as I looked at her. Walking over to her, I noticed she was also using. And so we took it again together. Her name was Caroline, and I later found out she was 16. I wound up getting her number that night, and we eventually started dating. Dating, though, really consisted of us hanging out and sleeping together. I'm not sure why her parents never stopped us, but they were cool with it. She was my girlfriend, but she wasn't my only girl.

If a girl wanted me, I would give myself to her. I went to parties and sold drugs and did things I couldn't always remember the next day. And by the end of my freshman year, I hated school and wanted to get the heck out of my mom's place and my town.

కావావా

Mom had a friend who told me about a co-op in Texas where college students lived and worked together. She explained it as a great opportunity to live in community with people and attend college. It sounded cool enough, and I'd certainly felt I had missed out on the stereotypical college community. So, I decided to move to Austin and attend a community college there for my sophomore year of school.

I left without saying goodbye to Mom. My buddy Jacob and I loaded up the car and took off, leaving San Antonio in the dust. The co-op consisted of about 100 guys and girls. The place had been built in the '70s by a bunch of peace-loving hippies. It was a clothing-optional community, and when Jacob and I arrived, we saw a bunch of naked men and women walking around. We took my bags to my room and wandered to the music venue where a lot of local bands and parties took place. As soon as we opened the door, we were overwhelmed at the combination of loud music, alcohol, drugs and nakedness. All around, people were just doing some weird stuff. And Jacob and I looked at each other in a little bit of shock.

"Dude, Eric, this is really weird."

"Yeah, man. It is. I don't know if I'll fit in here."

"Good luck with this."

Jacob left me, and I stood there letting the reality sink in. I was living in a nudist community. I was living there alone.

ॐॐॐ

"Go to your rooms!" A man dressed like Oscar the Grouch from *Sesame Street* screamed at our group of new house initiates, adding multiple expletives. He stood in front of us wearing a tin trashcan and a painted green face. Glancing around the room, I noticed everyone was in a weird costume. There were pirates and painted faces, all worn by men and women who were anything but sober. I scrambled with the other new community members to my bedroom and lay on my bed. My face was painted blue, and as I lay on the sheets, I could hear yelps and hollers from the drunken cohorts downstairs. Soon, they made their way to my room. The door swung open, and I was surrounded by a group of yelling party animals.

They brought me a large bottle of alcohol and forced me to chug it from the bed where I sat still.

"Chug it!"

"Whoooooooo!"

"Yahooooo!"

"Chug! Chug! Chug!"

The liquid stung and made my throat and chest feel warm as it went down. I coughed and put down the bottle, various members grabbing my elbows and arms. They all began to chant as they swept me away into a sea of people.

"One of us! One of us! One of us!"

やややや

Each week, community meetings were held. Most of the time the people who showed up were intoxicated and high — randomly yelling yea or nay to decisions being made.

School was not a priority, and I began scheming any illegal way to make money. Living in the co-op made it easy. I had access to almost any type of drug I wanted. And the deeper I got into drug experimentation, the more terrifying my days and nights became.

I was at a party in the house the first time I used the psychedelic drug DMT. Everyone doing it sat on a couch listening to weird music. But using it only made me feel like I hadn't gotten enough. So my buddy and I went downstairs and bought $10 worth from a green-haired guy wearing a skirt.

Back in my bedroom, I tried it again. I sat down and put it in a bong, lighting it and holding the smoke in my lungs for 10 seconds. I stood, walking out to the patio right outside of my room. And in an instant, it was as if my whole life dissolved.

It's not really a feeling you can explain to someone — what tripping out really feels like. But I felt as if everything around me had transformed into a digital world, like I was Zordon from the old show *Power Rangers*. My body didn't feel real, and it didn't feel attached to me. Hunched over, I kept calling out, "Oh, my gosh, I found it. Oh, my gosh, I found it."

I was terrified. My friend could tell something was up and not right. He shook my shoulder, trying to coerce me to come back inside.

"Dude, what's up, man? Come back inside."

I bent over, rocking back and forth, and began to legitimately freak out.

"Eric, what's up, man?"

"Dude, is this real? Who are you?" I continued to rock back and forth.

"Yeah, man."

"Is this forever?" Panic began to overwhelm me. All around, people also using DMT were doing crazy things. Suddenly, I let out a deep and ear-splitting scream.

"Hey, you're back," someone from the crowd said.

I was back, but I was terrified. And I eventually knew I wanted out.

Backstage Pass

❧❧❧

At the end of my sophomore year, I decided to move back home and re-enroll at the San Antonio campus of the University of Texas. I went back to working at the restaurant, but I knew I didn't want to live with Mom again.

So, when Caroline's parents offered to let me live with them, I hesitantly accepted their hospitality. They were good to me. They bought me food, gave me money and treated me like a son. And when they left the house, I'd sleep with their teenage daughter. I was still hooking up with other girls at parties and doing drugs, though I had cut down significantly from my days in the co-op. Eventually, Caroline discovered I was being unfaithful.

"You're just so sketchy. I know you're always doing things behind my back."

"I'm so sorry. I'll quit," was my reply.

But I didn't. And while we were still dating, I felt it was eventually time to move out. It took me a while to get settled into an apartment with my friend Brad. I lived with an older alcoholic woman from the restaurant for a while. But I had grown so disrespectful of people and property that she eventually kicked me out.

I had just begun my third year of college when Caroline's mom asked me to help Caroline with her math homework.

"Caroline, come on. I'm trying to help you, and you're not even trying."

She lay sprawled out on the floor, petting my dog and begging for attention.

"I don't feel like doing math, Eric. Let's do something else."

"I'm here to help you do your homework. You've got to do this." I was not in the mood to mess around. She got up, her hair hitting her shoulders, and left the house. Shortly after, I got a phone call.

"I don't want to be with you anymore, Eric."

I later found out that she was seeing someone else. His ring hung on a necklace I had given her. And while I had never maintained any degree of faithfulness during our relationship, I somehow thought that at the end of the day, Caroline would always be there. She would be the one I'd be with in the end. My chest filled with sharp pains — the kind that make it hard to breathe in and out. And so I did the only thing I knew to do. I partied it off.

❧❧❧

I stood alone on a table, swaying senselessly to the cover band as my head filled with terror from the hallucinogens I had taken with my friends back at the co-op. I was visiting for the weekend. Jumping off of the table, we danced in an insane circle of people. We raised our beers up into the air like we were toasting immortality. In the middle of a dance, I felt a sharp pain in my foot. Walking off to the side, I saw half of a glass beer bottle sticking into the bottom of my foot. Blood gushed heavily as I pulled the shard out. Blood began to seep onto the floor, pooling in a dark, widening stain. I tapped some girls on the shoulder, and they looked down at my foot.

"Hey, that's blood."

"Can someone help me?" I shouted.

One of the girls started filming me as I begged for someone to find a bandage for my foot. The girls, high, walked away. I wandered into the street, walking in a circle and reaching a point of severe panic as each person chose to ignore my request for help.

"Help me! Someone, please help me." Panic and tears seeped out of me. I could hold it in no longer. "Help me!" Eventually, a girl took me inside and found a bandage, but during that period of time, I legitimately thought I was going to die. *Why am I trusting these people? No one here cares about me. I need to start caring about myself.*

భావా

After the party at the co-op, I decided I wanted to start seeking spirituality. I had always believed that a God existed, though I didn't know exactly what I believed. And I didn't know much about the God the Christians believed in. And I didn't have any idea of what he might want to do with me. A friend of mine gave me a book he had been reading called *A Peaceful Warrior*, and I guess I liked the idea of that, being a peaceful but strong person. Close to the beginning of the book, it talked about how fasting can often bring spiritual clarity. And what I wanted more than anything was peace. The memories of moments where I was high or experiencing hallucinations were terrifying. They haunted me like a grim reaper — constantly following me, ready to steal my life and joy. I figured that it wouldn't hurt to try a fast. I knew fasting was a part of a lot of different religions, and in all of them, it seemed to bring some sort of peace of mind.

On the second day of my fast, I walked into my organic chemistry lab and noticed a new girl across the room. She was beautiful, but I didn't lust after her the way I had with so many other girls in the past. I noticed she was struggling with her lab work, and I walked over and started talking with her. Her name was Addison, and she possessed this sort of innocent disposition. Her eyes lit up with a joy I didn't have. By the end of it, I had made more of a mess than I had been helpful.

"Hey, do you like Italian food?" I asked her as we began cleaning up our station.

"Oh, yeah, love it."

"Well, I happen to know of a great Italian restaurant." I told her about where I worked and asked her if she'd ever want to grab dinner.

"Sure," she said, smiling.

I told the guys at work I was bringing a girl that next week.

"Treat her right. She's a great girl," I told them, wanting everything to go as well as it could. Dinner was great, and afterward, we headed to my apartment to play a game of cards. In the middle of our evening, she told me she was going to go swing dancing with some of her guy friends.

"I'll see you later! It was great hanging out tonight, Eric." And she grabbed her coat and left. I sat there in a sort of daze. I had never been around someone so innocent — where dinner and a game of cards didn't turn into something more. Over the next few weeks, I found myself wanting to spend more time with Addison. I was drawn to the steady person that she was. Our friendship grew, and I was thankful for the influence she was having on my life. Though I still didn't know who he was, I prayed to a God I believed was up there in the sky somewhere. "If you keep this girl in a relationship with me, I will change. I promise I'll change."

Change doesn't come easily, though, especially when you've been traveling down a path of self-destruction for so many years. Addison invited me to attend church with her, and though I was not a devout follower of Christ, I began to understand God as a merciful God. I began to see that God did not want to punish me for the unfaithful, empty person I had been. He instead wanted to love me, despite the things I had done.

Addison showed me the same mercy. She accepted me and loved me the way Christ loves. We were continuing to grow closer, but we never once crossed a physical boundary. I wouldn't say we were seriously dating, but she was the one I cared about. Our relationship was strong, and it was built on more than physical interactions or sex. And yet, despite that, whenever I'd see other girls, it was like my flesh cried out for them. I was constantly being tempted and tested, and I failed more than once.

One day, sitting in my apartment alone, I heard a little voice in my head I can only believe was God. *What about Addison? Is she important to you? Because she's not going to be with someone or put up with someone who is unfaithful.* I dialed her number and hung up three times. Finally, I let it ring and heard her voice on the other end.

"Addison, I haven't been faithful to you," I said, cutting to the chase.

"Really? I can't even imagine you doing that."

"I'm really sorry. You don't deserve that."

"Well, thank you for your honesty."

"I'm so sorry."

We didn't talk for four days and then I called her back. I knew she was the only one I wanted to be with.

"Addison, I want to be with you. I will not be unfaithful to you again if you give me another chance. You deserve someone who is going to be faithful and dedicated to you in a relationship. I can be that person."

"Okay." And in her answer was more grace and mercy than I had experienced in my whole life.

❧❧❧

The more I grew to love Addison, the more I began to love this man named Jesus. I never really knew anything about him, but in the beginning months of our relationship, the Bible became so real to me. It's like I'd been living in a box, hiding away my secrets and deceptions. I had been seeking empty love — a love that leaves when the sun comes up and doesn't satisfy your aching heart. In Christ and in Addison, I found great love. Merciful love. Love that forgave even the darkest parts of me and my past. For the first time in my life, I wanted to be open and honest about who I was and what I desired. My heart didn't change overnight. I still struggled with alcohol and so many other things, but I saw a change as more and more Christian men and women began entering my life. One in particular, a strong Christian man named Phillip, became my closest of friends. He actually baptized me on my birthday as I made a public declaration of faith in Jesus Christ. Each day I seemed to hear a small voice in my head saying, *Follow me, and I will give you fullness of life.* But I still had much to learn about following Christ.

After graduating from college, I applied to Oregon State and miraculously received a full-tuition scholarship into the graduate school of engineering.

I was nervous to leave Texas — particularly the community of Christian friends I had developed there. I was moving to a completely new state, and I didn't know if I could make it on my own.

I saw how God provided, though, when I stumbled upon Kings Circle Assembly of God. I'll never forget the first time I visited. I was immediately welcomed by everyone I met, and the message that day was about being open to the ways that God can work in our lives. I heard a message about how God isn't a boring God — how he will always surprise us with what he can do. I felt right away that this was where I was meant to be.

I longed to get involved, and before I knew it, I was meeting with an incredible group of men weekly to pray, offer encouragement to one another and simply live life together. It was a community that changed my life. They showed me what it looked like to be a man of God. They showed me what it looked like to walk with Christ — to be a part of a community of believers.

I could never have dreamed of living in a more beautiful place than Oregon. One autumn weekend, a bunch of us set out to a men's retreat — also referred to as a "men's adventure." The notorious Oregon rain began to fall, hitting the windshield as we drove down Highway 101. After a while, we turned onto an inconspicuous gravel drive and pulled up to a beautiful home overlooking the ocean. The sky was painted black. You couldn't see the waves hitting the shore, but you could hear them. They sang a song of rest and comfort.

The next day, after sharing our life stories, crabbing and lounging around, we drove north to play a couple games of mini-golf. As we drove, I thought about Addison.

The sky dipped into the water as I looked out upon the stillness, and I couldn't help but think about how God had provided for me. In all of it, though, Addison wouldn't leave my mind. Leaving Addison in Texas left an ache inside of me. She was the person I wanted to share these experiences with. I wanted to tell her how the water made me wonder at the power of our creator. I wanted to share with her the conversations I was having with the men I was growing close to in the church ministry. I wanted her to be there every day to share every experience with me. There, staring out at the water, I decided that what I wanted more than anything in the world was to make Addison my wife.

అఅఅ

It was the day before my wedding, and I found myself sobbing in a hotel room, replaying the conversation with my lifelong friend Gunner in my head.

Gunner had been living in France when I announced Addison and I were to marry. The day I told him, he insisted he would fly back for the wedding and stand beside me as a groomsman. I was elated. We had been through so much together. It felt right that he should see me make one of the most important decisions of my life. It had been years since we had seen each other, though, and when he arrived the day before the wedding, he was strung out on heroin, his eyes looking empty. Sitting across from a friend who had always been like my brother and seeing how void of joy he was sliced open my heart and made me realize how similar I could have become if it had not been for the relentless love of Christ.

"You look dead, Gunner. Spiritually dead." He looked up at me and just stared.

"I know. I know, man."

Great Love

Crouched on the floor of the hotel room, my Christian friends Phillip and Andre listened as I shared my concerns about Gunner and prayed that somehow God would do a good work in my friend. I wanted him to know the love I was experiencing. And as we prayed, peace slipped in like fog in the early morning. It rested upon our shoulders, and it calmed me. It was a peace that did not go away, even as we got in the car and drove to the ranch where I would marry the great love of my life.

Sitting in the front seat of Phillip's car, I hunched over sobbing in deep and raspy breaths. But I was not crying because of pain or burden or emptiness. I was merely overwhelmed by the presence of God. I looked over at Phillip and whispered, "It's not about me. It's all about Christ and his love for me."

I found myself so full of love as I drove to marry my bride. Not only love for the most incredibly gracious and merciful woman, but love for a Savior who filled my empty heart with complete joy.

He had given me great love — full love. And I was willing to follow him anywhere.

Real Healing
The Story of Dianna
Written by Stefanie Potter

I didn't see it coming. I never would've left had I known. I was in Portland for a concert when my aunt called me.

"What do you want?"

"Your mom collapsed, Dianna," she reported.

I gasped. "What? Is she okay?"

"I don't know. She's in the hospital."

My stomach sank, and I nearly dropped the phone.

"They've got her hooked up to machines. She's not responding."

I barely choked out, "I'll be there soon," before I doubled over and burst into tears.

I frantically stumbled to my car and rushed back home.

Three long days passed. I sat by her hospital bed for hours on end, heartbroken at the sight of my mother, drained of life. Mom was never very healthy: She smoked, was overweight and had diabetes. But she was only 40. *How can this be happening?*

The doctors made it clear that she would never recover. My family had to make one of the most difficult decisions of our lives — to let her go. They took her off the machines, and her body shut down.

It was all over. I went home in a haze.

I collapsed onto my bed, feeling weak and hopeless. After a few hours of heavy sobbing, Dad came to my door. I avoided eye contact.

"Go away!"

"I have a meeting with the funeral director tomorrow. You can come or not come."

I stayed curled up and silent.

I started thinking about my future. A sudden fear overtook me. I crawled to the phone and called my friend Sue.

My whole body shook.

"There's no way I can live here anymore. I *can't* be alone with this man," I told her.

"Come to my sister's house. I'll leave right now to pick you up there."

I sighed in relief. "I'll be ready."

I threw my stuff in bags and darted out the door.

And never returned.

❧❧❧

I grew up in Lebanon, Oregon, back when it was a small town. Everyone knew everyone else's business, and yet in the '70s, family issues were still considered private matters. Dad benefited most from that fact.

Dad appeared to most as a respectable man, working hard to care for his family financially. We had a lovely three-bedroom home with a fireplace, but to me it felt like anything but safe or cozy. I left early and stayed late after school every day to avoid being home. My teacher was the only one who always treated me with kindness.

Dad hurt me repeatedly throughout my childhood.

For some reason, Dad chose me to be his punching bag. Rather than protecting me as a father should, he beat me up whenever he was angry, which was often.

He also sexually abused me ever since I can remember. He'd sneak into my room and force me to do horrible things that made me feel sick. I couldn't hold back tears whenever Dad hurt me like that. I hated him.

After one encounter, I remained curled up on my bed, staring him down with disdain.

"I *hate* when you do that to me."

"You're fine," he said as he buttoned up his shirt.

"No, I'm NOT." Tears rolled down my face. "I'm telling."

He walked over to me and stroked my head. "Dianna, I told you this is our little secret. We don't tell secrets," he said sweetly.

I pulled away and slapped his hand away. "I don't care anymore! I'm going to tell the police on you."

Suddenly, things got serious.

"You listen to me, little girl," he demanded as he grabbed my shoulder.

"Ow!" I tried to pull away, but my tiny arms weren't strong enough.

He moved right up into my face. "If you tell anyone, I *will* kill you."

My heart skipped a beat. I could barely breathe.

He pushed me down as he let go. He turned to leave.

"Mom will help me," I mumbled under my breath. He heard me.

"Yeah? Good luck with that. She can't protect you if I hurt her first."

I lay there for hours, shaking and crying. I hated to see him even yelling at Mom, and I *never* wanted to be the cause of her pain.

I felt like Mom and I were close. I'm pretty sure Mom loved me, although I don't remember her ever saying it. If Mom knew what Dad kept doing to me, she never let on. I'm sure he kept her afraid, too.

Years later, he reminded me that his threats were serious. He took out his 30-30 rifle and pointed it straight at me. It scared me to death. Of course, I complied with his demands.

కాకాకా

When I was just 11 years old, Dad impregnated me. He refused to live with the consequences of his vile actions, so he beat me up until I miscarried. My parents took me to the hospital to get everything "taken care of." I was too young to understand what went on.

Even throughout all that, nobody — not even the doctors — did anything to help me. My older sister lived in foster care and my younger sister hated me, so they didn't help, either. For all I know, he may have been abusing them, too, and keeping us all silent.

I felt all alone.

Although Dad's threats continued, I tried telling people. I even tried to turn Dad in to the police, but it didn't work.

I wanted to die. I tried to overdose, but I was unsuccessful. I ended up in the hospital instead. I begged the hospital staff not to send me home, so they sent me to stay with my uncle. After I tried to overdose again, the hospital staff released me right back home with my dad. I felt trapped.

Every summer, I flew to California to visit Grandma. When I stayed with her, I finally felt like I'd found a place I could be safe.

But my beloved summer visits ended when a guy who rented out the back house found a way to take advantage of the young girl visiting her grandma. He and another guy raped me. My hideout suddenly became unsafe; I felt there was nowhere to turn.

The rape, added to my ongoing abuse at home, made me feel even worse.

Am I only good for guys to use? I will never be loved.

ᕬᕬᕬ

I was only 19 when Mom died. The only person who I thought might actually love me left me too early.

The night she died, I drove to meet my friend Sue at her sister's house. Sue had a hard life, too, and I knew she understood. I stayed with Sue and Ann for days, bawling my eyes out for most of it. I pictured Mom with her curly hair, red cheeks and the beautiful smile that made her whole face light up. I remembered how I could make her laugh even when I angered her. It seemed nobody else in the world knew how great of a person she was; she wasn't educated or accomplished by the world's standards, but she was helpful and beautiful from the inside out. I missed her already.

Ann had a stash of drugs. I'd never tried more than a little pot and beer before then. I wanted to numb the pain so badly that I joined her in using them. I don't even know exactly what I used; I just kept going. I do know I ended up hooked on meth after those days.

᠀᠀᠀᠀

I stayed on meth, alcohol and a little pot, seeking to cover up the pain. *I'll be fine,* I thought; but I wasn't.

I got a job at a Circle K, but after five months the management fired me for being on drugs. My life was a mess.

Every time my body wanted more, it felt like a life or death situation. I didn't have any money, so I traded sex for meth. I hated my life; I often prayed to die.

I lived paranoid and depressed. I spent many years cooped up in my house with blankets covering the windows. I stayed up into the early morning hours almost nightly, keeping watch.

ಎಎಎ

My life lit up a little when I met Paul. He was a sweet-talking Mexican man I met one night at a bar when I was 29. We started dating, but our relationship ended quickly. He left me after he got me pregnant.

I stayed away from meth during the pregnancy to keep my baby healthy. But after Angela's first birthday, I started at it again. By then I had child support payments coming in from Paul, which helped me support my child *and* my habit. I sent Angela to my sister's a lot and to Paul's when he'd allow it. That way, I could use meth when she wasn't around.

ಎಎಎ

I let my dealer live with me for a while, which made the drugs even more accessible to me. That all ended when a neighbor called the cops with a child endangerment claim. They came and raided my house. They opened the safe and found everything. They didn't arrest me, though; they only wanted my dealer.

I finally went into treatment.

Treatment seemed to be going well, until I learned my drug and alcohol counselor used meth herself. She went to jail, and I relapsed, *hard.*

ಎಎಎ

Five years later, I finally decided to try to get clean again. I entered New Beginnings outpatient treatment and Narcotics Anonymous. It actually worked this time! I learned how to let go of drugs and alcohol and started to feel freer than I'd ever felt before. I acknowledged that I depended on these things to cover up the pain of my past, rather than dealing with the pain in a way that was good for me. I didn't want to, but I knew I needed to start addressing the real and difficult issues of my life.

They talked a lot about spiritual things in the treatment groups, and I began to take an interest in learning more. After a couple years of treatment, I joined a Bible study that some people there recommended. Mom had me go to Sunday school at a church as a child, but Dad held a deep prejudice against people who believed in God; he always said it was a scam. But the people I met in the Bible study seemed genuine and kind, and it seemed like their faith in God made a positive difference in their lives. *Dad abusing me all those years was the real scam.*

Unfortunately for me, the leaders canceled the Bible study group after a little while. But I wouldn't give up.

I approached a woman named Beth about my disappointment in the cancellation. I didn't know her at all, except for the fact that she led the Chi Alpha campus ministries in Corvallis.

Beth had a glow about her. It wasn't just her blond hair, that she dressed nice or had a pleasant attitude. Something was different about her. She had genuine hope in her eyes, and I could see that she cared, deeply.

She was thrilled to come alongside me. Beth and I started meeting regularly to study the Bible together. The Bible drew me in and made me feel like I missed out on something amazing all those years. I never thought I needed God before, but as I learned more, I realized that I actually *did* need him.

❧❧❧

Beth invited me to church. I agreed to try it out. Sunday morning, I entered Kings Circle with my 11-year-old daughter next to me; we both had butterflies in our stomachs. As people by the entrance greeted us with warm smiles and handshakes, I let out a sigh of relief. We walked in and slid into a pew next to Beth and a few other people I'd met before.

The pews were filling up, but there wasn't an overwhelming number of people. I gazed around and saw photos of people from different countries across the walls. *I guess they're open to different people. That's good.*

A band started to play upbeat music on the stage up front.

"Good morning! Welcome to Kings Circle," the leader said into the microphone. "God is good, and he loves us. Amen?"

Everyone shouted, "Amen!"

"Would you join us in singing praises to Jesus, our king and rescuer?"

Everyone around us stood up, so Angela and I stood

up, too. They all sang along with the band to a song I'd never heard before. I listened and clapped along.

The singing continued for a while, going from song to song like we were at a concert where everyone knew the words. But instead of the band performing for the crowd, it was like the crowd all joined the band, singing with passion to God.

I read the words as they all sang around me. People were closing their eyes and expressing the words like they really meant what they were singing — thanking God for how deeply he cares for us, acknowledging God as the one in charge and crying out to God for help.

As they sang, I felt my entire body start to tingle like something filled it with goodness. It was an amazing feeling. I suddenly realized — *Jesus is real!*

After the service, I told Beth about how I felt during the music.

Her eyes lit up with excitement. "That's the Holy Spirit," she explained as a smile flashed across her face.

"What is that?"

"Well, you know that God is our father — the good and loving kind, not the abusive kind."

"Yeah."

"You know Jesus is God's son who came to pay the price for everything we've done wrong, so when we accept his gift, we no longer need to fear the consequences of our bad past choices."

"Yeah, I believe that."

"Well, because you believe that, God sent you the Holy

Spirit today!" She stopped a moment to figure out how to explain it. "The Holy Spirit is the part of God that lives inside of you now. He's there to make you brand new. The Holy Spirit will help you to become the person that God made you to be."

"Whoa …" I sat for a moment trying to understand it all. "Well, I like the feeling!"

"Feels like pure goodness inside of you, right?"

"Yes, exactly."

"Well, friend, your adventure with Jesus is just beginning. I'm excited for you!"

I smiled.

On the ride home, I wondered about what Beth meant. *I guess God has something in mind for me.*

"Mom?" Angela interrupted my thoughts.

"Yeah?"

"I liked it there. Can we go again?"

I looked into my little girl's brown eyes and smiled. "Absolutely."

ও৵৵

As time passed, Angela and I became more involved at Kings Circle. I joined a Wednesday night group led by Pastor Steve on learning how to pray. I learned that because of what Jesus did for me, I could talk to God about whatever I wanted, and he would listen. I started talking to him about my past. I didn't want to address it, but I knew I needed to.

I felt like the Holy Spirit started urging me to deal with the issues behind why I relied on drugs in the first place: being abused and feeling unloved all those years. I started counseling again.

Since I started addressing my pain, I even found and joined Bible studies and classes and groups on healing from sexual abuse. It was all so helpful in my journey toward healing.

It wasn't easy to deal with my past, but it was worth it. Although I always felt alone and unloved, I learned that God was always with me and loved me more than I could understand. I believe he even remained with me during my abuse, and his heart broke over it even more than mine did. I believe he's still with me, and the Holy Spirit is inside me, helping me to heal from it.

I no longer needed to depend on drugs to mask the pain; instead, I depended on God to help me work through the pain and be healed. Life was so much better leaning on Jesus.

The feelings of depression and self-pity that used to keep me hiding out for long periods of time no longer controlled me. There were still days that I struggled and wanted to hide, but I learned to give those feelings to God to deal with, and he helped me bravely face the days so I wasn't trapped in those feelings for too long. Whenever I felt like I was going to fall, he always came through for me.

My relationships improved, too. I used to cuss at people and judge them harshly; I stopped doing that. It's like God took those urges from me. I prayed for people regularly, since I'd experienced the changes that God brought about in me.

I used to fight with my daughter all the time, but we started getting along much better. She also was changed by God. She became a junior leader in church, and I felt so proud of the young woman she was becoming. People always said what a good daughter I had. She went through a lot of struggles with me. I knew her life would've looked very different had we not let Jesus into our home.

God even led me to forgive Dad. I hated him for nearly 40 years. I used to plot how to kill him. I never thought I'd have the strength or desire to talk to him again, after leaving home at 19. But God changed my heart toward him.

"I think I need to go see my dad," I confided to Beth one Sunday afternoon. Pastor Steve had talked about forgiveness during the church service earlier that day. "He hurt me deeply, but I know God wants me to not hold it against him anymore."

She looked into my nervous eyes and slowly nodded.

"Would you go with me?" I looked away, realizing how awkward the question probably sounded.

She placed her hand on my shoulder. "I would be honored to."

So we went.

Dad had been in a nursing home for a while.

The staff walked us to his room, and I started to shake more with each step.

We stood there for a few moments and waited.

My body calmed down, and I suddenly felt brave. "I'm ready."

She nodded.

I walked in first. "Hi, Dad."

He looked startled. He lay in bed and made a noise that sounded vaguely like my name. "Yes, it's me, Dianna, and my friend Beth. We came to see you."

Beth and I sat down. He did not look good at all. His health problems clearly limited him. He couldn't even talk.

I didn't know what to say, so we all sat in silence for a while. He didn't look at me much.

When a few minutes had passed, Dad tried to say something. I couldn't understand him. I just tried to look at him kindly, so he knew why I was there.

Although it was a quiet visit, God healed something inside me as I sat there. I looked at the man who once caused me such horrible pain and actually felt compassion for him. I realized if God could love me, God could love him, too. He did not want Dad to hurt me, but he loved both of us enough to want our lives to be changed for good. "Dad, I want you to know that I love Jesus now. He is changing my life and healing me from the pain of what you did to me. That's why I'm here. I never thought I'd come visit you, but here I am."

He looked up at me, seeming to ponder what I just said.

"I'll be back to visit you again, Dad."

He nodded and looked away.

Beth and I prayed together before we left.

Just as Jesus demonstrated his love for those who don't care for him, I finally felt free to love the person who did the least loving thing to me.

ॐॐॐ

I started to feel so alive. It amazed me that I could genuinely praise God even with my difficult past and the influence my dad had on me. But I knew I had a loving father in heaven, Father God, who was taking care of me.

I joined some other people in my church in getting baptized in the Willamette River, demonstrating how Jesus cleansed me from my past and gave me a brand-new life.

I started attending a Wednesday night group on parenting with about 10 other women, some of the most amazing women I'd ever met. I really enjoyed it.

Laura led the group. She possessed that same beautiful glow about her that I noticed in Beth. Although it was a group on parenting, Laura led us to do whatever we needed to do, like we were working through life itself together. Sometimes we read the Bible together and talked about what it said, and other times we just chatted and played games. Sometimes we talked about what was going on in our lives and prayed for each other. Everyone there was real and honest with each other, but always in a kind and loving way. It still tripped me out a bit how genuinely loving they all behaved toward me, especially compared to how people treated me growing up, but it was something I decided I could definitely get used to.

Beth trained me to lead the same "Discovery" Bible study that she led me through a couple years before. I started leading it with one woman, and I found myself looking forward to God touching more women through me in the way that he reached me through Beth.

I realized that God kept me alive all those years for a reason. I still didn't know exactly why I went through the struggles, but I did believe that God was healing my pain and encouraging people through me.

Completely Satisfied
The Story of Lisette
Written by Amy Jones

This wasn't at all like the commercials — they made it seem like the potential parents wait happily in anticipation for their answer. Me? I sat alone in my parents' hollow bathroom, and as the two pink lines popped up, I instantly screamed, "You're 17 and pregnant!"

Yep, it felt quite a bit more dreadful than the imaginary couple on TV made it seem to take a pregnancy test.

Now what? Will I finish high school? Is this man going to stick around? What are my parents going to say?

❧❧❧

I was the kid in the middle. Not the unpopular *Diary of a Wimpy Kid* type, but definitely not the popular Barbie doll, either. I enjoyed the simplicity of being plain old, everyday, average me. That was, until the middle school cafeteria got my friend Monica Ritter thinking. She decided we needed to become popular. "I don't think that's a good idea, Monica," I said, but she insisted we at least go sit at the popular table. My nervous, shaking hands practically made the Jell-O jiggle right off my lunch tray. The closer we got to the table, the more certain I became that this may not be a good idea.

Much to my surprise, the popular kids liked me. They rallied around me so much, I hardly even noticed Monica getting pushed farther and farther toward the end of the table. I'm not sure why they took a liking to me over her, but as I pursued my budding reputation as a popular kid, some contrary instinct in me joined them in making Monica feel worse each day. I began leaving her out, pushing her aside, making fun of her clothes, calling her names and using any cutthroat gesture I needed to keep the popular kids wondering what I would say or do next. I remember thinking Monica's plan for popularity had backfired in her greasy pizza face.

My willingness to betray Monica's friendship earned me the right to privy and sacred information within this group. I was the first to know when and where the Friday night parties were. I earned extra points for encouraging my new friends to come with me to the mall before the party. I flattered them by expressing how great they looked in the latest fashions, and they faked similar affirmations back. Once our egos were pumped to the height of invincibility, we covered for one another. Hiding the garments in purses and in coats, each girl took turns stealing her eveningwear. I felt guilty at first, but the popularity payoff made it all seem worthwhile. Why those clothes were so important, I will never know — we partied in the dark. No one appreciated how cute we looked, nor did anyone have time to care between the alcohol and groping advances.

I continued partying and stealing during the week. On

Sundays, I reluctantly accompanied my parents to church. I hated it. They could tell, but were at a loss. Their fires of anger and frustration grew as my attitude and behavior worsened. I needed to dampen the flames. Agreeing to attend church summer camp, I figured, would do the trick.

As the days began to get longer, summer quickly approached. It was finally time to leave for camp. *I am going to show these goodie-goodie kids what it means to be popular.*

We crested the hill a few hours after sunrise. Picturesque visions of cabins, trees and perfect children lay just beyond the camp entrance. Turning this camp upside down was my secret mission. For the next week, I would pull no punches and teach these prudes an unofficial curriculum — plugging up the camp toilets with paper towels, creating a popular table in the mess hall, throwing spit wads during Bible time and becoming familiar with the basics of disrespect and lewdness. By the time camp concluded, most campers had turned rebel. I felt sweet satisfaction as parent after parent picked up their children, oblivious to the hidden monsters I'd created.

ॐॐॐ

Ninth grade would prove to be my best (worst) yet. I had my heart set on attending a particular middle school. My parents didn't know why, but I had my eye on Chad

Hill. I hadn't seen him since seventh grade, but I heard he was going to that school in the fall.

"Come on, Mom, I think it would be good for me to change schools."

"I don't know." Her face showed skepticism.

"I won't get into trouble there. I promise. Just let me go," I begged.

"Okay, but no more of your shenanigans. You have to get serious about school."

"Oh, I will."

The first day of school, I dressed in my best stolen outfit. I hyper-vigilantly searched for Chad down every hall. There was plenty of time to make my "cool" mark, but finding Chad came first. Skipping class, I found him outside fighting. After the crowd dispersed, I sauntered toward him.

"Hey! That was a great fight."

"Dang, Lisette, I haven't seen you in a couple years. You look good."

"Thanks." I was flattered. "Maybe ... we could hang out sometime."

"Yeah, that'd be great. There's a huge party this Friday night. It's gonna be a rager. Lots of weed, tons of booze and maybe us skaters can corrupt some preppy kids, huh?"

"Now that sounds fun. I'll see ya there."

Occasionally, I attended class. One day, I was tossing books in my locker when Amber stopped by. She definitely was not in our "cool" group. I had talked to her a few times, but that day, she approached with a certain confidence and invited me to her church. I agreed. I felt rebellious because she didn't attend a church like my family did, and I figured my parents wouldn't like that.

But something about that church experience changed me. I liked it, and I wanted to go back often. It was nothing like the church my family attended. The music jived to a contemporary beat. People approached with smiles expressing gladness in seeing me. Their eyes sparkled with joy. They spoke of Jesus like he was a friend.

Growing up, I would slip out of the service and head to the bathroom in the basement. I felt like Jesus' presence was there, and I danced privately with him. After a few of these encounters, I began to wonder, *Why is everyone upstairs in church when Jesus is down in the basement?*

The people at Amber's church seemed to know the basement Jesus. I left her church excited to share everything with my parents.

I could barely spit it out. "… and then, and then, I just knew this was the real Jesus. I want to keep on meeting him. I want to go back with Amber this Sunday and to youth group next Wednesday. This is just what I needed. I am so happy and feel so free."

Scowling with disappointment, they finally spoke.

"You will not go back to that church. It's not the faith you were brought up with. You turned your back on everything you've been taught. You're no longer allowed to talk with Amber, and you are certainly not allowed to go back to that church. It's our church or nothing."

My heart balled up in my throat. Before my eyes could tear up, I ran to my room and locked the door. For hours, I stared at the ceiling, vexed and angry. I wouldn't emerge until I had a plan, a direction. I plotted and schemed to twist the knife in their hearts like they just twisted it in mine. Finally, it came to me — I would make such bad decisions, my parents would give up on me. I'd be blatantly disrespectful with an "in your face" approach.

As a result, the ante was raised at school. The things I used to do for acceptance were about to hit the next level. Now, it was smoking pot on top of the drinking, theft, cussing, disrespect and cigarettes.

Chad and I were sneaking out and getting drunk, the world at our fingertips. We met at the bar. Chad would hang back, while I stood outside soliciting for a buyer. Once we secured our alcohol, we slipped into the park and wherever else we could get wasted and high. My parents tried to ground me, but nothing worked. I was a short, petite blond tornado focused on destroying my parents' lives.

The next mission became skipping school, stealing my parents' car and joyriding all day with my friends. That thrill got old, so I sought the next level.

"Hey, guys, let's skip school today and ride in style."

"What are you talking about, Lisette? Your parents' van isn't exactly the tightest ride."

Pulling a spare key from my pocket, I looked around to see if anyone caught on, but I saw only blank stares back.

"Guys, this is the key to Kylie's parents' car."

"What? Lisette, that's crazy. You know their family's out of town. We can't steal their car."

"Exactly, their family is out of town. All the more reason *to* steal their car," I muttered as I took a drag off my cigarette.

We hatched a plan while walking to Kylie's house. I worked for serious reputation points that day. Mostly, I was annoyed Sara couldn't stop laughing. Beth wasn't exactly quiet, either, with her constant, loud whispers of "Be quiet!"

I led the heist, calm and cool. Unlocking the doors of Kylie's parents' car, I instructed everyone to get in and shut up. Between their noise and clueless slamming of doors, they could have woken a hibernating grizzly. We soon discovered we'd done just that. Kylie's parents had hired a house sitter. Our ruckus and stirring in the driveway piqued his curiosity. He tried chasing us as we drove away, but to no avail. We got away. *Now what?*

We needed to lay low, so I drove to a friend's house, and we chilled for the rest of the day. About two hours later, we heard a rap on the door.

"Police. Open up."

Panic stricken, we obeyed.

Wide-eyed and full of regret, we complied with returning the car to avoid arrest. Although this was alarming, it wasn't quite enough to stop my tornado's destructive path. A plan began forming in my brain. If I was really going to flex my "cool" muscles, I would need to up the shock factor. I would host a house party while my parents were asleep upstairs. This would twist the knife in their hearts.

"This is a great party, Lisette. I can't believe how many people came. Your backyard is the perfect place to have a party. I can't believe we haven't used it before."

"I know, and my parents are so dumb, they're clueless we're out here."

"It doesn't feel like it's four in the morning. I am so drunk right now."

"I think everyone is," I slurred as I took another guzzle while looking at my watch.

Lowering the beer bottle from my lips, I caught a glimpse of Mom standing on the threshold of the patio.

"Lisette Rachel Parsons, what do you think you're doing?" she yelled, hands firmly at her hips.

My friends quickly jumped our fence in a paranoid frenzy. In a matter of seconds, it was just me and Mom standing amidst the trash and empty beer bottles. The party music still played in the background. *Awkward.*

"Did you think we wouldn't catch you?"

I paused. *Was that a rhetorical question?*

"I got up to go to the bathroom, and I heard a noise coming from the backyard. I looked out and saw at least 20 teenagers partying. Really, Lisette? Really? When are you going to learn? Turn off the music. You're grounded from everything."

Something about her tone made me realize she was serious this time.

The next Friday night, I woke up to someone calling me from outside my bedroom window.

"Brandi? Is that you?" my groggy voice scratched as my eyes tried to make out the figure at my window.

"Of course it's me. Wake up. A bunch of us are going up to the Bald Mountain cabins to party. Come with us."

"I can't, Brandi. I'm in trouble from last weekend's party."

"You have been in trouble before, and that never stopped you. Chad will be there. I know you want to come. Now get up. Let's go."

I thought, *I guess I'm gonna have to get firm.* "I can't go. You don't get it. This time I'm in real big trouble. Now go away."

As Brandi turned away, I began to reminisce with fondness over those cabins and the time we siphoned gas to get up there. How we broke in to party and play house. It was a fun night. I'd swept the floor, *swish-swush*, sipped my beer and proclaimed, "One day, we will live here, you guys." I dreamed those cabins were ours. I loved them, but I knew I couldn't go.

The next day, I made a rare appearance at school. Campus was abuzz with gossip heard from miles away. I was mobbed upon arrival.

"Did you hear?"

"Hear what?" I questioned.

"Some kids broke into the Bald Mountain cabins last night."

Tell me something I don't know.

Probing for more, I asked, "What exactly happened?"

"There were four kids up there. They just went crazy. They vandalized toilets and smashed TVs in with bats. An owner of one cabin caught them as he pulled up to the cabins. He called the cops and held the kids at gunpoint until the police arrived."

I stood there speechless. *That could have been me. My life needs to change.* As a result, Chad and the three others were sent away to boys' and girls' homes.

❧❧❧

I worked at Hot Dog on a Stick in the mall the summer after my junior year of high school. A guy I knew was supposed to meet me there after my shift. Once I'd realized he'd stood me up, I decided to make him jealous by finding another guy to hang out with. Immediately, a guy walked by that looked vaguely familiar. I knew I had met him somewhere before, I just didn't know where.

"Hey!" I yelled from behind the counter.

He cautiously approached. "Yeah?"

"Do you want to hang out tonight?"

"Sure."

I later learned his name was Calvin, and he was the go-to guy for party locations. He was a drug dealer — major "cool" points with my friends.

The end of the summer brought the beginning of a new day at high school. *What to wear? I got it, that skirt I just bought.* Looking cute, I busted through the high school doors ready for whatever my senior year would throw at me. As I crossed the threshold, the wind blew my hair so perfectly around my face I could have been in a shampoo commercial. Just about the time I looked around to make sure everyone saw me, I puked all over the freshly waxed floors. Mortified, I quickly ran home.

The next day, I wore the same cute skirt. After all, no one got the chance to appreciate it on me the day before. Looking just as cute, I busted through the high school doors ready for whatever day two of my senior year would throw at me. This time, my hair blew straight across my face and in my mouth as I promptly puked in the exact same waxed spot. I went home again.

I don't get it. I have never been allergic to anything in my life. How could I be allergic to this skirt? Maybe I need Benadryl. I wept as I mourned my fashion loss. Once my mom figured out what was going on, she suggested, "Lisette, maybe it's not the skirt. Maybe you're pregnant."

After a Kmart run and trip to the bathroom, the pregnancy test stick revealed my fate. There we sat — just me, Mom and two unwavering pink lines. As we waited to tell Dad, there was a knock at the door. It was Calvin. Without a word, I handed him the plastic baggie that held the clue to our future.

He just stood there in shock.

Then there was that awkward moment when Dad got home. "So, did you get your 'sickness' under control?" he asked, with a knowing look.

I think the stress must have gotten to me, because I

burst into uncontrollable laughter and replied, "Not for another nine months."

After I'd regained my composure, Dad had few words for me. "We all choose roads in life, and you just chose a hard one."

Abortion wasn't an option, but adoption was. I started the process for a closed adoption through an agency. They sent me a caseworker to explain the process and to discuss potential adoptive parents. I called her with my questions, and she brought me profiles each week of families interested in raising the baby growing inside me. In my immaturity, the only important qualification I had was that I wanted my baby to live on a farm.

I lay in bed at night unsure if I was making the right decision.

"God? Is adoption a *yes* or a *no*?" I prayed again and again without knowing the answer.

When I was seven and a half months pregnant, my caseworker walked through my door with a smile and a briefcase announcing, "I found the perfect family. They are everything you've been looking for."

As I looked further into their profile, I felt like a two-ton brick hit me in the chest. That was it. I knew. I couldn't go through with this.

"Nope," I sputtered indignantly as I threw the papers across the table. "I can't do it. I will raise him myself."

With that, she was gone. By April, I had completed all my courses to graduate high school and given birth to my son Miles.

Completely Satisfied

~~~~~

I always loved music. As far back as I could remember, singing was part of my life. As much as I dreaded going to church with my family each Sunday, it did afford me the opportunity to sing.

Some of my fondest childhood memories are of me and Dad singing at the old folks' home on Tuesdays. It was fun to see the residents' faces light up as we sang. We built relationships with them and each other.

When I was 10, I tried out for and was accepted into a traveling children's choir. I was thrilled to participate. Those times of innocence and music were who I really was before everything went awry.

I never felt close to God at church. I regarded him as a distant power who was my best friend when life was going well, but my worst enemy when it wasn't.

Once I found out I was pregnant, I cleaned up my behavior. My new friends became the kids in my choir class. They seemed to still enjoy the beauty and innocence of music. My love for it began to return. *Music can still be a part of my life.*

~~~~~

After high school, life felt uncertain. I didn't fit in at college with my friends, but I wasn't prepared to be a mom, either. I lived at home the first seven months of Miles' life. The party scene still found me, yet no one understood me anymore. I didn't even know who I was.

At 20 years old, I had just earned my associate's degree and was still open to anything life threw my way. I met Sebastian, but didn't like him much. Still, hanging out with him gave me something to do. He filled his days with smoking pot and photography. In March, he went west for a spring break road trip. I didn't give it much thought, until he called me one day.

"Lisette, I love it out here. No, seriously, it is beautiful. I am dropping out of college to move here."

"Are you serious? Why would you do that?"

"Move out here with me. Let's make life happen."

Something about the way he said, "Let's make life happen," stirred a yearning in me to agree to go west with him, no matter the cost.

Everyone I knew argued against this move. Sebastian was *not* a good guy. Their concerns about my move were warranted, but my stubborn heart decided to go.

In the back of my mind, warning signs kept popping up. My family's church regularly participated in prayer vigils, which entailed praying for nine straight days to ask God for something specific. I did just that. My request? For God to be with me in Oregon.

The day of the big move arrived. I packed my Toyota 4-Runner to the brim, squeezed Miles and myself in and took off for Ashland. In a matter of two weeks, Sebastian called off our relationship, leaving me sobbing and shaking with regret in the middle of the living room floor as my son screamed out the window of his room, "Help me!"

I thought, *My sentiments exactly.*

The tornado tore through my life again, leaving a new path of destruction. I felt like all I had to show for 20 years was a mess of brokenness.

Prior to our breakup, Sebastian introduced me to his cousins Dave and Donna. I liked them right away, but he thought they were weirdo Bible thumpers. Dave and Donna were the only people besides Sebastian who I knew in Oregon.

We began hanging out together, and I realized going to church was pretty much all they did. They went to church on Monday, they went to church on Wednesday and they went to church on Sunday. Miles and I began to go with them. We had nothing better to do.

Dave and Donna attended a church in Medford, Oregon. It was the polar opposite of my religious upbringing.

I was used to ritualistic ceremonies. Their church was relationship oriented. I knew sitting, kneeling and standing, over and over in Mass. During their worship services, people raised their hands and jumped with excitement. I knew formal and polite. Their church members seemed intentional when they said, "So good to see you." I grew up reciting The Lord's Prayer. These people called out to God with deep emotion.

What is wrong with these people? I thought. Dave and Donna asked if I was "saved" and "baptized." *What are they talking about?* Irritated, I shot back an, "I grew up in church, okay? Back off." I thought I had all the answers.

Dave and Donna's church created a love-hate feeling in my heart. On one hand, I loved the way they sang and the words of their songs. But they would talk about something called the power of the Holy Spirit. Honestly, it freaked me out. The words *Holy Spirit* took me back to a lock-in event at church when I was a girl. They showed the movie *The Exorcist.* Whenever anyone mentioned the Holy Spirit, I would immediately get fearful and think of that movie. Goosebumps formed from the back of my neck to the skin on my calves. The words of *The Exorcist* danced their way back into my mind: "If someone speaks in a language no one knows, he or she is of the devil." To me, if the Holy Spirit made you speak a different language, that was of the devil.

Yet, there was this girl who sang on the stage at Dave and Donna's church. She raised her hands sometimes, knelt down in adoration other times and acted like it was just her and God in the room. I wondered if the Holy Spirit had anything to do with her actions. What she did on that stage didn't look "of the devil" to me. She looked so fulfilled, joyful and happy. I was thoroughly confused.

Attending church with Dave and Donna started to become commonplace. As our relationship continued to develop, they offered to watch Miles so I could attend the upcoming Encounter Weekend. I had no idea what that was. They told me it was an event where I stayed at the church all weekend to "seek God." Immediately, I was turned off. I didn't want to go, but Dave and Donna signed me up, anyway.

As the Encounter Weekend approached, I asked a random guy in the lobby one Sunday, "What is this thing like?"

He told me, "It's like getting hit by a semi. It's crazy, but it's soooo good." I just stood there, dumbfounded.

All I could spit out was, "That's helpful. That doesn't tell me anything." I thought the guy would be somewhat sympathetic. He just grinned.

As he walked away, I made out his muffled words, "Who cares? Just go to it."

Alrighty, then, I guess I will just "go to it."

By the time Encounter Weekend rolled around, I had made up my mind. I was going to be open to whatever happened. Little did I know what that would mean. The evening session on Friday challenged us to ask God to show us the movie of our life. *What does that mean?* Back to my sleeping bag I went. I just lay there halfheartedly talking to God in my head.

"Okay, God, show me the movie of my life."

Nothing.

A few moments later, "Come on, God, just show me."

Nothing.

A few more minutes passed. "Show me! Show me! Show me the stupid movie of my life."

Again, nothing.

I got mad. This weekend was not starting off well.

I slept off the fury and dragged myself to a session called "Breaking Soul Ties" on Saturday morning. We were given paper and pen and instructed to write down names of past unhealthy relationships. My mind became clear, and I began writing name after name. Five minutes passed, and I was still writing names. The next step was to go around the circle and individually call out the names one by one, each time saying, "*Person's name*, I give back anything I have taken from you, and I take back anything I have given to you. I break this soul tie in the name of Jesus." It was a powerful experience. I physically felt the weight of my past relationships falling off me. It was also a humbling experience, because after going around the circle five times, most people came to the bottom of their lists. I still had 45 people remaining on mine.

Saturday afternoon, I went to another session that touched something deep inside me. We wrote down our various sins and struggles, nailed them to a cross and later burned them. During that time, we identified what was taking hold of our lives. We could raise our hand, and someone would pray for us. I realized I had a lot of things I was battling. I raised my hand, and the others prayed for me.

As Saturday came to a close, I felt like I couldn't stop staring at my ugly self in a mirror. Before that weekend, my eyes had been blinded to many things. There was more to live for than myself and my desires. I felt freedom and excitement welling up inside me. I began to experience a long-lost feeling — joy.

Even though these positive experiences were happening in a way that seemed out of my control, I hung on to my resistance to two things: baptism and the Holy

Spirit. There was no way I was going to let these people convince me either one of those was for me.

After breakfast, Sunday morning brought a boring time between the end of weekend events and people arriving for church. I sat in a cozy corner of the church with my Bible in my lap. I decided to close my eyes, flip it open and stick my finger in a random spot. My eyes became peeking slits as I peered through, making out the Book of Matthew. I opened them the rest of the way and discovered my finger was on a verse where Jesus asked John the Baptist to baptize him. The words that followed began to jump off the page at me: "Allow it now to fulfill all righteousness." *I am not getting baptized. I was baptized as a baby. I am saved. I will not.* Again, I read: "Allow it now to fulfill all righteousness." It deeply spoke to me, as if it were the voice of God. *I can't do it.* "Allow it now to fulfill all righteousness." *Dang it! Fine! You win. I have to get baptized. I know this is from you, God.*

The pastor got right to business as the church service started. He called anyone desiring to be baptized to raise his or her hand. I raised my hand with certainty, and before I knew it, I looked out among a sea of people. Time stopped for me as I scanned the room, only to find Dave and Donna beaming with joy from the front row. I felt overwhelmed. I paused and relished the moment.

"Lisette?"

Snapping out of serenity, I broke my gaze and came to.

"Lisette, would like to say anything before I baptize you?"

"Well, I think I really do want to say something. Because of this weekend, I realized I blamed God for everything. I blamed God for the things I've done wrong. I now realize it was my choices that were causing me to be mad, not God. I want to be a disciple from here on out. I am sure of that."

After church, the pastor invited people forward to be prayed over. He called it "being filled with the Holy Spirit." *Oh, no! Anything but that. I can't go there. It's "of the devil."*

I didn't know what to do. I thought about running out. If I went forward, I might end up speaking in tongues, and that seemed disgraceful. My parents spoke in tongues, but I never let them do it in front of me. *If something like that happened to me,* I thought, *I couldn't live with myself.*

About the time I started walking away, something caused me to turn back around and walk to the front. As weird as this "being filled with the Holy Spirit" sounded, it was my last stumbling block in a long line of obstacles I had overcome that weekend. I was still committed to my original plan for the weekend, to be open to whatever God wanted to happen. So, I began to get prayed over. The remaining shackles of my old life fell to the ground, and I began speaking in a different language. I didn't know if this was speaking in tongues or not, but it was very liberating and felt wonderful. I jumped around and raised my hands as the music began to play. I had the sensation of being brand new. I was never again going to be the Lisette I had been.

For the next two weeks, I could not stop speaking this other language. It got so bad, I had to take time off work until the foreign words coming from my mouth started to settle down. When I returned, I still uttered and mumbled in tongues under my breath. My co-workers hardly recognized me. They told me that I looked the same, but nothing about me was the Lisette they once knew. My parents eventually found out about my Encounter Weekend. At first they thought I'd joined a cult, but after flying out to meet with my pastor, they gave me their blessing.

Shortly after Encounter Weekend, I joined the church worship team. I found a way to start using my gift of music again. I didn't realize how much I'd missed singing until I started singing again. But my participation in the worship ministry was short-lived.

A few weeks after I began, I decided to step down. Pride and my relationship with Sebastian became a hindrance for me, and I felt like God wanted me to lay down music until I could deal with these hurdles in my life. I believed God asked me to stop singing. I came to believe that God wanted me to give singing up because I was too full of pride. I knew it was the right thing to do, and I felt God was leading me toward a more honoring life. I realized that my relationship with Sebastian was separating me from the life I was supposed to live. Singing would have to go. I had old dead branches in need of pruning before my tree of life could proclaim God's goodness through singing and worship.

Sebastian still lived next door. He still came over, we were still "friends," we celebrated the holidays together and we were still attached. I still occasionally fell into temptation with him. This caused a fierce war to wage inside me. I desperately wanted to live like Jesus, but I knew I had to let Sebastian go. I told him our relationship wasn't working out. He wouldn't listen. I refused to party with him. He didn't care. We didn't share the same friend groups. That didn't bother him. He wouldn't get out of my life. That's when I decided to move from Ashland to Corvallis.

This move would be a final break from Sebastian. It felt empowering to have my own plan, independent from a man. I decided to get my degree from Oregon State University. I moved. Sebastian followed. *Why?* Neither of us was happy. He still cheated on me. He still partied. I did not.

My life was headed in a completely different direction.

ﻬﻬﻬﻬ

"God, I am dead serious. You have got to get Sebastian out of my life. I want to follow only you, and I can't with him. Amen."

I wonder why Sebastian hasn't called for a few days? That's weird.

Checking Facebook, I received a message. The sender's profile picture looked like Sebastian taking a "selfie" with a girl on his lap. Curious, I opened the message.

Dear Lisette,

You're probably wondering why you haven't heard from me in a few days. You were right. We are over. I have met the woman of my dreams. A few days ago, I went surfing and had a near-death experience. My whole life flashed before my eyes. When I got to the beach, this beautiful girl was standing there. It was like she was waiting for me. I am in love. Thanks for the past five years. Good luck with life.

Sebastian

That message sure looked to me like God's answered prayer. I was thankful but devastated. Five years was a long time. Rather than running to alcohol or parties, I allowed myself to feel the pain of his rejection. I was not going to try to fix it. I was going to do something different. I was going to worship God through it.

I did just that. I stumbled upon a song called "Divine Romance" by Phil Wickham. A line in that song said, "In your presence, God, I'm completely satisfied." It spoke to my heart. I didn't feel like I was completely satisfied in the presence of God, but I knew in my heart I was. I just kept repeating those words aloud over and over again, "In your presence, God, I'm completely satisfied. In your presence, God, I'm completely satisfied."

Miles got older and more handsome with each passing year. That degree from OSU became a reality. I continued to trust God and to see evidence of him continuing to do great things in my life. I joined Kings Circle Assembly of God Church in Corvallis, which led me to a very supportive small group. They loved me at my worst and were always so happy to see me. They made me feel wanted and needed. They also held me accountable if I missed a week of meeting together.

Four years after I felt God tell me to stop singing, I felt like he gave the gift back and asked me to join the worship team at Kings Circle Assembly Of God. Once I felt him telling me to pick it back up again, I was nervous. Just the thought of being too prideful made me timid. At first, I would sing so quietly, they didn't think my microphone was on. I was careful to use singing in a God-honoring way. I had finally learned what true worship was — not a feeling or a show, but a way of life.

❧❧❧

I knew life with Jesus wouldn't be easy, but it beat anything I had been through. I thanked God for healing the pain and sorrow of my past. He continued to play an ongoing concert in my life where every song became one of my favorites. The words of each song were beautiful, but the chorus remained the same, "In your presence, God, I'm completely satisfied."

Free at Last
The Story of Lynne
Written by Onyih Odunze

Crack! The noise reverberated through the car.

"What was that?" I asked no one in particular. I knew that distinctive sound; after all, we'd just been shooting at target practice. But I was confused. *Why did it sound like a shot had been fired* inside *the car?* Andrew's face looked just as perplexed.

A gunshot? Who had been shot?

Scared, my heart thumped in my chest. I turned around to check on my sister, make sure she was all right. I twisted toward the backseat and called out to her.

"Lillian. Lillian? Are you okay?"

Silence.

Desperate for answers, I peered into the backseat. All I knew for sure was that I heard a shot. *Was my sister shot? Or had she done the shooting?*

The answer to that question changed the course of my life. Nothing was ever the same.

❧❧❧

I was born in San Luis Obispo in 1947 and grew up in a blended family with four siblings and two half-siblings from my father's previous marriage. My mother helped raise my half-brother and half-sister, so they were always around, making our small house even more cramped.

When I was a young girl, people referred to my mom as "Indian Princess," because she had traces of Cherokee in her lineage. Dad was a chef, and Mom was a waitress, which seemed fitting.

Mom carried a few extra pounds on her petite frame. Dad's weakness was something altogether different. He drank. A lot.

My father's fondness for alcohol made my childhood very unstable. We traveled all over the place when he got a whim, sometimes surviving on chicken noodle soup and canned spaghetti from the Salvation Army. Once, we stayed in Barstow, California, for two weeks during which a nearby cave doubled as our bathroom.

One hot summer day, my brother, sister and I got home after a day at our lemonade stand and found our mother nursing a black eye.

"You've got to get away from him, Ruby," Aunt Julie told Mom.

Mom sighed, ran a hand through her dark hair. "Oh, Julie. I don't know."

"What do you mean, you don't know? You wanna hang around until he kills you? Or until he moves on and starts on the girls?"

"You know, Daniel isn't always that bad," Mom countered, her words floating on a soft sigh. "It's almost like he's two different people. He's fine six months out of the year, and the rest of the time, he flips."

My mother loved my father, but she was also scared of him. So was I. We all were. The fear that blanketed our family was palpable; it was almost like an extra member of the household.

My father wasn't just physically hurtful to my mother and brother; he also had a way with words.

"Pick up your feet, quack quack." It was one of his stock phrases, and he said it to all of us, even Mom. I was never sure if he was teasing us or mocking our slow pace. Either way, his words had the desired effect. I always flushed and walked a little faster as my father laughed.

☙☙☙

"Quickly, Lillian! We have to leave soon," Mom called as she tried to hurry us along. She had finally decided to leave my father and was taking me, my sister Lillian and my brother Alex with her.

We rushed out of the house and took the bus to my older brother's house. I was 7 years old.

Matt welcomed us with open arms. "It's good to see you, Mom. Here, let me take those for you."

His tight hugs belied his casual welcome, and I knew he was glad that we were no longer under Dad's abusive control.

Counting Matt's wife, Erin, and my niece, there were seven of us in the house. I felt safe at Matt's house, somewhat free of the pervading fear that I had known all my life. After nine months, we moved out and got a little place of our own.

"Mom, maybe you can get some help?"

Mom was silent for a moment. "You mean welfare?"

Matt nodded. "Yes. I don't think you can make it without some kind of assistance."

So, my mother sent in an application, and we got on welfare when we moved out of Matt's house. However, there was a condition attached: Mom couldn't work until I was at least 11 years old and Lillian was 13. In those days, the welfare authorities preferred to have at least one parent at home with the children, instead of away at work.

Things changed after we left my brother's house. Away from Matt's supportive presence, Mom started drinking.

It started simply enough at an evening out with relatives. My aunt and uncle passed through town every now and then, and they always stopped for a visit with Mom. They would drink beer, but Mom always drank soda.

"Hey, Ruby. Have one on me," Aunt Julie offered one day.

Mom shook her head. She still lived with the memories of my father's alcoholism and its effect on our family.

"I don't drink."

"A little beer isn't going to hurt you."

Somehow that argument won Mom over, and one little drink that evening turned into a chronic battle with alcohol.

❧❧❧

"Hey, what's up, Jenny?"

My mother had been dating Owen for a long time, and it looked like they wanted to make things permanent. Owen had two daughters — Jennifer, who was a little older than me, and Valerie, who was younger. I'd gone to visit Jennifer. I spent a lot of my free time with Owen's daughters, and their apartment was one of my hangout spots.

"Nothing much. Wanna go in my room and listen to some music?"

"Uh, maybe later. I'll just watch some TV."

"Hey, Lynne," a male voice said.

I turned toward the voice and recognized Brian, a man who lived in the same apartment complex. I was used to seeing him around.

"Hi, Brian."

Brian and I chatted casually for a few minutes while Jenny was in her apartment. After a while, he convinced me to come out to his truck, so he could teach me to drive.

"Sure, I'll just let Jenny know where I'll be."

I called out to Jenny that I was stepping out and would be back in a little while. True to his word, even though I was only 10 years old, Brian did teach me to drive. He also molested me.

One day, I was driving Brian's truck, and Owen's two daughters were in the vehicle with us. I was going too fast and ended up hitting a telephone pole. The car was smashed up really badly, and so was my face.

"Oh, my goodness," Mom gasped when she saw me. "Whatever happened to your head?"

Shamefaced, I kept my head down, and an easy lie sprang to my lips. "I, um, I got in a fight with some other girls."

"Lynne! You know better than to fight. Come here, let me take a look at that."

I spent a lot of time with Lillian and Jennifer and their friends. Being around older girls got me doing things I shouldn't have been doing at my age.

One day, some girls invited us to their church. We went, and something about the message and the music moved my sister and me. At the end of the service, we went forward with others and asked Jesus into our hearts.

We had the best intentions, but they were swept away in the company of my older friends and our quest for fun.

❧❧❧

The tendrils of smoke that curled up from her lips captured my attention, and I couldn't help staring at the streetwise 21 year old who lived in a trailer home near Owen's apartment.

She winked at me. "Wanna learn how to do this?"

"Yeah, sure." *Why not?* I was sure she didn't know how old I was because I was tall, always wore makeup and looked mature for my age. It didn't matter to me. She taught me how to inhale, and I was hooked. I started smoking at 11. At 14, I started drinking.

I felt like a grownup and started doing grownup things. I developed a crush on Andrew, who, at 21, was quite a few years older than me. Although he wasn't officially my boyfriend, sometimes we did make out. He also could provide easy access to alcohol whenever I wanted it. This fact came in handy whenever we needed beer for one of our little gatherings.

One day, Andrew wanted us to go somewhere for target practice, so I invited Lillian.

"Um, I'm not sure about today, Lynne," she demurred. "You know I still have to talk to Jake."

Jake and Lillian had been dating for a while, and things were pretty hot and heavy with them. I knew Lillian suspected she was pregnant and was worried about breaking the news to Jake, her 20-year-old boyfriend. At 16, she was two years older than me and far too young to be a mother. The worry lines on her face worried me, and I would have done anything to take them away.

"Come out with us, Lil. You can ask Jake, too, and maybe you guys can talk there."

Undecided, she shook her head. "I don't know."

"Come on. It'll be fun, you'll see," I countered, pushing her to say yes.

A reluctant smile lit her face, and she nodded. "Okay. I'll ask Jake."

I whooped in excitement. "Cool! Andrew will come by to pick us up."

A few hours later, Andrew's shiny new Impala pulled up outside my house, and we piled in like a pair of carefree teenagers with nothing more on our minds than sun, fun and beer.

               ক্ষ্ণক্ষ্ণক্ষ্ণ

I threw my head back and laughed. I was young, free and having fun. The warm, sunny day, my sister, the guys we loved, alcohol and laughter — what more could a girl ask for?

Never mind that I was only 14 years old.

I fanned myself with my hand, a futile attempt to alleviate the heat. I passed my cold can of beer back and forth in both hands, then rolled it over my forehead.

"Hey, it's my turn to shoot," I called to Andrew.

"Aw, boys first, sweetheart." A cheeky grin lit his face as he tossed the gun to Jake.

Andrew sank down on the grass beside me and reached into a cooler for a can of beer. We were in a small canyon, close to the woods, taking turns shooting at distant targets.

Bang! A shot rang out, but instead of whistling off in the distance, it clanged off metal. Andrew glanced over at his car and jumped to his feet, seemingly unaware of the can of beer that flew out of his hand.

"Jake! What are you doing? You shot my car?" Andrew's brand-new 1961 Chevy Impala was his pride and joy.

Stunned, Jake glanced down at the gun in his hand and backed away, contrite.

"Hey, man, I'm sorry. I didn't mean to. I'm really sorry."

Andrew grabbed the gun from Jake and walked around the car, checking for any damage and muttering to himself. The sight of the bullet hole upset him, and he threw Jake's gun in the glove box and got in his car.

The rest of us eyed each other and decided to join him. It was clear that our target practice was over for the day.

We grabbed our beer and piled into the car. I sat in the front passenger seat next to Andrew, while Lillian and Jake sat in the back. Andrew spun the dial, and the deep voice of Johnny Cash enveloped us.

We spent a few minutes drinking beer, listening to music and making small talk.

"Hey, Andrew," Jake called from the backseat. "Mind if I get my gun back?"

Andrew opened the glove box, pulled out the gun and handed it over. "Sure."

I smiled at Andrew as I drank. He lived close to a bar and was old enough to buy drinks for the rest of us. Even though we had never been intimate, I enjoyed hanging out with him and engaging in the occasional make-out session. I was glad Lillian had agreed to come out with us. She hadn't wanted to come, but I had talked her into it, and from the way she was giggling behind me, I could tell she was enjoying herself.

Crack!

The noise reverberated through the car, startling me and interrupting my musings. I bolted upright.

"What was that?" I asked no one in particular. The look on Andrew's face told me he was as confused as I was.

Scared, I turned around to check on my sister.

"Lillian. Lillian? Are you okay?"

Questions raced through my mind in the few seconds it took me to fully turn around.

Then I saw her.

Or rather, I saw the hole in her chest. Curiously, there was little blood, and a part of me wondered why as my brain tried to make sense of what I was seeing.

Lillian was sprawled across Jake in the backseat, a neat hole in her chest. Jake held her, a stunned look on his face.

"What happened?" I screamed at him. "What did you do? What did you do to my sister?"

Desperate to reach her, I tried to scramble into the backseat. "Lillian! Lillian, wake up, wake up!"

Andrew pulled me away. "Lynne, Lynne, stop."

I grabbed his arm. "We have to get her to a hospital. Now!"

Frantic, he nodded and started driving.

Yes, we needed to get to a hospital. They would save her. I needed to believe that my sister would be just fine.

❧❧❧

The three-mile ride to the hospital was excruciating. Time crawled as we dashed down the freeway, with my sister's body inert in the backseat and the rest of us frozen in shock.

At some point, a sliver of sanity wormed its way through the haze, and I started throwing the beer cans out the window. My sister and I were both minors; we couldn't be caught with alcohol. Plus, I didn't want to get Andrew into trouble; after all, he was the one who had bought the beer.

When we got to the hospital, we put Lillian on a gurney and wheeled her into the hospital ourselves because no one from the hospital came out to help us.

Waiting for word on Lillian's condition felt like the longest hours of my life. I kept reliving what happened inside the car. My thoughts went back to Jake asking Andrew for the gun.

Had it really been an accident? Had Jake shot my sister on purpose? Could she have pulled the trigger? She'd been planning to tell him that she was pregnant. *Maybe he knew and got angry or scared and decided to take care of the problem? Or maybe she got scared?*

My mind bounced all over the place, and I didn't know what to think. I had no answers. All I could do was hope that my sister would be all right.

Soon, a doctor came out to speak to us, a solemn look on his face.

"I'm sorry, but there was nothing we could do."

Nothing they could do? My sister was gone? It was difficult to wrap my head around the fact that I would never see her again. I had just been with her, and I could still taste the lunch we'd shared a few short hours before.

The police came then, put me in a police car and took

me to a home for delinquents where I sat in a room for a few hours. They later took me to the police station and tested my blood alcohol level.

We didn't have a telephone at home then, but someone got word to my mother. They went by the house and broke the news of Lillian's death.

"Where's Lynne?" she asked the messenger, frantic and scared that I was also hurt.

When they found out where I was, she and my stepfather walked all the way to the police station to get me. Her relief at seeing me was short-lived. Lillian was dead. *My sister was dead.* The doctors couldn't save her life. And I felt like it was all my fault.

The police returned my sister's personal effects to my mother, and we walked home, each of us locked in our own private misery. My mother clutched Lillian's things to her chest, as if they were a priceless treasure. Silent, I walked beside her, full of grief and guilt.

દેન્દેન્દેન

"You were with someone who is 21?" my older brother raged at me.

I was crushed at the look in his eyes. I loved my big brother, and the fact that he was angry with me made me sad. But, he was right to be upset. I had no defense. I had talked Lillian into going out with us. My "boyfriend" bought the alcohol. What did it matter who I was with or how old he was? I alone was to blame for the fact that my sister was gone.

Those months after Lillian's death were incredibly difficult. I was burdened with guilt. I burst into tears at odd times.

I picked up the last picture of the two of us together. My mom kept it displayed on the TV at home.

She's dead. Lillian is really dead.

The thought was too much to bear. In addition to self-condemnation, fear became a constant companion. I couldn't stay home alone. Oppressed by feelings of self-blame and scared out of my mind, I tried everything I could to drown my sorrows. I drank, I smoked, I went out dancing whenever I pleased.

Once, I even stayed out all night without telling my mother.

When I got home the next day, I realized I had not been fair to my mother, and I resolved to do better from then on.

I met William at a dance, and we started dating. We both enjoyed going out to the beach for dances and impromptu music shows. Sometimes, famous musicians like Bobby Darren and Fats Domino would show up.

William didn't drink, and that helped me cut down on my drinking. He was a chef and often came to my house to whip up one of his specialties.

"What are you making today, Will?"

"It's Thousand Island dressing. It will go great with our salad."

Things progressed with William, and I knew he wanted to marry me. I wasn't so sure he was the right man for me. He was a very young 19 and often acted immature. But what sealed it for me was the way he acted when we went to the movies. He would always order a soda for himself, then turn around and ask me, "Want a drink, Lynne?"

Well, why couldn't he offer me a drink before he bought and paid for his own drink?

When I was 16, shortly after I broke up with William, I met another guy, Justin. I had gone dancing, and he kept asking me for a dance. I finally agreed, and we started talking and ended up talking almost all night. After the dance, he asked me to meet him at the beach the next week. I agreed.

We got married five months later.

પ્લ✑પ્લ✑

Our son Dylan was born in 1965. Justin was in the Air Force, and we lived off base in Santa Maria, California. One day, a few weeks after our son's birth, my husband came back with a letter in his hands and a strange look on his face.

"What's wrong?" I asked.

He waved the letter at me. "I've been called up. I'm going to Vietnam."

I gasped. I knew it was not outside the realm of possibility that he would go to war; he was in the Air Force after all. But, with an infant son, I was reluctant to let him go. Reluctant and scared.

"How long will you be gone?"

He shrugged. "Probably about a year."

I nodded. It was a bit much to take in. *How would Dylan and I cope without him?* My uncertainty must have been written on my face because he slipped his arms around me and held me tight.

"Don't worry, honey. I'll be okay," he muttered into my hair. "Maybe you can go visit my mom for a while. Just for some company."

I considered his idea. It would be a little strange going to spend time with someone I didn't know, even if she was my mother-in-law. However, the thought of being alone with Dylan was unappealing.

Justin was from Upstate New York, and his mother, whom I had never met during my two years of marriage, still lived there. So, a few weeks after my husband left for Vietnam, Dylan and I packed our bags for the long trip to New York.

ॐॐॐ

Still bleary-eyed and clutching Dylan in my arms, I looked around as I walked onto the plane. Being on an early flight to New York, I was still feeling the effects of too little sleep.

I smiled at my neighbor and took my seat. The airplane that day felt like a veritable rainbow, with people of different races populating the aisles and seats: Caucasians, African-Americans, Hispanics and Asians.

The hum of conversation surrounded me as the plane taxied onto the runway, then took to the air.

Gradually, the chatter turned to God and wondering what race he was. I had only ever seen pictures of Jesus as Caucasian, so I did feel he was white, but other people had different ideas.

"Maybe he is as black as me," an African-American man in a nearby seat piped up, chuckling to himself.

An olive-skinned woman across the aisle joined the conversation. "Jesus is a Spanish name," she said, pronouncing Jesus with an "H" sound. "Figure it out."

"I tell you, Jesus was no white man. Not Hispanic, either. He was Jewish. We all know Jewish people have dark skin," someone else contributed.

The good-natured debate continued, and I found myself thinking about God. I remembered going forward at church as a little girl, but nothing much had come of that. Justin and I didn't go to church, but we did say a simple bedtime prayer every night. Occasionally, we would talk about God, but it never got serious.

What race is God? I was curious, yet I wondered if it really made a difference. *If he was white like me, did that mean people of other races couldn't come to him?*

Still tired from my early morning, the sounds of conversation faded as I drifted into a halfway place between sleep and alertness.

Suddenly, I felt a bump, and the plane shuddered. I sat upright and held my son closer. I didn't fly much, so I had no idea whether it was normal or not. A few moments of calm had me ready to relax, when the plane heaved again. The seatbelt lights blinked on, and the captain's monotone voice droned over the announcement system.

"This is to inform you that there's a snowstorm up ahead. We should be landing in a while, but it may be a little rough. Please return to your seats, and keep your seatbelts on."

People who had gone to the restroom or those simply stretching their legs in the aisle hurried to their seats and belted themselves in. The flight attendants checked each row to make sure we were all seated, then belted themselves in for the landing.

I felt the plane dip as if we were going to land. I would be relieved to be on firm ground again. But that didn't happen. Instead, the plane nosed up once more, and we stayed in the air.

Another announcement told us the plane was having problems with the landing gear. Fear curled in the pit of my stomach. *Problems with the landing gear? What would happen to us if we couldn't land? What if the plane ran out of fuel with all the circling we were doing? Would we just fall out of the sky?*

My heart lurched with the plane as it bucked and pitched angrily, buffeted by the snowstorm. The anxious murmurs of other passengers swelled until their voices filled the cabin.

What if we die here today? I asked myself. *Where will I spend forever — heaven or hell?* Our earlier discussion about God prodded me, urgent, demanding. In that moment, I knew that I was lost without God, and I felt certain that if I died right then, I would spend eternity far away from him.

Memories from the past flooded my mind: my drinking, the smoking, the guilt over my sister's death, but one image persisted — that of a little girl, walking to the front of a church and asking Jesus to come into her heart.

That little girl had become a young woman who sat on a quaking plane, her newborn son in her arms, and prayed a simple prayer.

Jesus, come into my heart, and make me yours.

A sense of peace enveloped me, and I basked in the knowledge that regardless of what happened on our flight, I was safe in God's arms.

❧❧❧

My mother-in-law was a certified nursing assistant who worked at a hospital. At first, she seemed happy to have us and was excited to meet her grandson. She lived in a small one-bedroom studio apartment, with a small alcove-type room attached to the back of the bedroom. Because Dylan needed to sleep in his crib, she offered us the use of her own room with its spacious bed, while she slept in the smaller space.

"Oh, we couldn't take your room," I protested.

"Don't worry about it. That's fine," she assured me. "You need the extra space for the little one."

Dylan and I slept in her room for a few nights, but I

felt so guilty about it that I insisted we swap places, and she agreed.

She had one regular visitor who came by the house often while we were there. I later discovered that she was dating the man, who happened to be married. Once, he came to visit, and she let him in while wearing her underwear. Her behavior shocked me and made me uncomfortable around her. Things got a little awkward, and I think she picked up on that, and her attitude toward me changed.

Not wanting to be a burden, I gave her some money to help with groceries and to buy me some cigarettes. Even though I had committed my life to following Jesus, I didn't yet know how to overcome my nicotine addiction. My mother-in-law smoked as well, so she was happy to oblige.

On her way home from the store one day, she stopped outside the door to talk to a neighbor.

"Your son's wife still around?"

"Yeah, she and my grandson are still here. It's all I can do to keep her supplied with cigarettes. Costing me a bundle," she said with a small laugh.

Hurt, I retreated into the room. *Why had she made it look like she was paying for my cigarettes, even though I had just given her a large amount of money?* I wondered what other things she was saying behind my back.

I miss you, Justin, I thought to myself. *I wish you would come home.*

The last straw was when I noticed that she had been going through my personal letters from Justin. Homesick and tired of her behavior, I took my son back home to San Luis Obispo.

ॐॐॐ

"What are you doing?"

"Getting ready for church," I replied to my stepfather. I had been attending church regularly since I moved back home, and I was doing well.

"Huh, church. They're just a bunch of pretenders, if you ask me," my stepfather huffed.

His comments hurt. It felt like he was belittling my efforts to pursue a better lifestyle, but I didn't let him deter me from the path I had chosen. Still, I felt uncomfortable living at home, and it became clear that I had to move.

I didn't have much in the way of resources, but I was able to rent a one-bedroom apartment. Even though it was in a seedy part of town, I felt confident that God would protect me.

After a while, I met a neighbor who was a retired preacher, and we struck up a friendship. He often helped me by driving me to the grocery store or to run errands. In return, I cooked two hot meals a day, which I gladly shared with him.

Our meals together were a great encouragement to me, and he always told me stories about the things God had done for him. Those talks gave me hope and strength when I struggled with various challenges.

I still missed my husband, and I was scared for him.

The news reports were full of soldiers dying and getting hurt in the war. I sent letters and care packages filled with scriptures and messages about God's love.

As fervently as I longed for my husband, I hoped and prayed that he would also come to trust God the way I did.

☙☙☙

During that time, I got friendly with Sue, a young mother who lived close by.

"Hello, Lynne," she greeted me with a smile early one morning.

"Hello, Sue," I responded in kind, as we exchanged pleasantries.

"Can you babysit for me today? I have to be at work."

I thought about that for a minute. I did babysit for Sue sometimes, but hadn't planned to that day. Instead, I wanted to attend a service with a famous female preacher, but as I considered Sue's request, I felt compelled to change my plans.

"Okay, no problem. Dylan and I will come by later."

We got home from Sue's house a little late that night, around 9 p.m. Exhausted, I readied Dylan for bed and tucked him in. Just as I was about to get undressed, the phone rang.

Who could be calling me at this time?

I dragged myself over to the phone.

"Hello?"

"Lynne, it's me, Owen. Mind if we come over?"

I hesitated. *What could be so important that my stepfather wanted to come over at this time of the night?*

He sensed my reluctance and continued. "I've got Justin here. He got back today and called us to pick him up from the bus station."

I shrieked in excitement. "Of course you can come over."

It was impossible to sit still. Justin was home! My husband was home. Silently, I thanked God for keeping me close to home. By going to babysit at Sue's, I was still awake and nicely dressed, instead of home and in bed.

I counted the minutes as time crept by, and finally, the doorbell rang. *He's here!*

Justin caught me up in a long hug and kissed me passionately, not caring whether we had an audience or not. Our reunion later that night was sweet, tender and intimate. Ecstatic that he'd survived and come home, I thanked God for his safe return.

Everything seemed fine, until he burst into tears. That was my first inkling that nothing was as it seemed.

❧❧❧

Mixed feelings roiled in me as I gazed at my sleeping husband. The initial sweetness of our reunion had soured over the many months that followed, and I struggled with the gradual suspicion that my husband had been unfaithful. His tears on that first night were alarming, but his subsequent behavior was downright suspicious.

Fighting my resentment, I spread a blanket over him as he slept on the couch. His insistence on sleeping in the living room, coupled with his coldness toward me, all reinforced my belief that he was having an affair.

My ministrations roused him from sleep. "What are you doing?" he barked.

Wounded by his tone, I stepped back. "I was only putting a blanket over you, so you can stay warm."

"Look, don't bother me while I'm sleeping, all right?"

I nodded wordlessly and went back to our room. It seemed clear that Justin no longer loved me, in spite of the fact that we'd had a second son and I was a few months pregnant with our third child. I had done my best to be a loving wife, but all my efforts were met with cruel, cutting remarks or brushed off entirely. *How much more could I take?* That night, I tossed and turned, praying and wondering what to do. I finally decided to confront him and ask him what was going on.

Mind made up, I drifted into a restless sleep.

৯৯৯৯

"Listen, Lynne. This isn't working. I plan to leave eventually, but I'm gonna hang around for a while," Justin said, casting a glance at my swollen belly. "At least until the baby is born."

Anger flowed through me. "Well, if you want to leave, then you might as well do it right away. You don't need to postpone your *plans* on my account."

A little while after Justin left, I wondered if I had been too hasty. *Maybe I should give us a second chance.*

I decided to drive over to Justin's job and see if we could talk. He cursed when he saw me.

"What are you doing here?"

"I only came to talk."

"We have nothing more to talk about."

Anger radiated off him, and I decided to leave. I had the boys with me in the car, and I didn't want to expose them to any ugliness. As I pulled around to leave, I saw Justin's red Volkswagen and noticed that there was a girl sitting inside.

I pulled up next to her and rolled down the window.

"Hi." I smiled to show that I meant no harm. "Do you mind coming over for a minute so we can talk?"

Her face closed. "I'm not coming over there."

"Look, I'm not going to do anything crazy. I have my kids in the car. I just want to talk a little. Please?"

She thought for a long moment and relented.

"So, you're Justin's girlfriend, huh?"

"Yes."

I nodded. It felt weird standing there and talking to my husband's mistress. "This isn't the first time he's done this, you know."

Her gaze sharpened as she caught the implication behind my words. "Really? What else has he done?"

A wave of pity swept over me as I looked at her. I wondered how long it would take before he started cheating on her, too.

I wrapped up our conversation, drove my children home and prayed.

Lord, I've done all I can to save this marriage. I believe it's time to let go. Help me, Lord. Help me to be strong.

❧❧❧

Justin and I got divorced after seven years of marriage and three children together. A few years later, I met and married my second husband, and our daughter was born in 1973. The relationship with my second husband was turbulent; he suffered from bipolar disorder, which made him loud, disagreeable and very volatile. Again, in spite of my best intentions, my second marriage ended in divorce after 12 years.

My biggest regret with my second marriage was the nonexistent relationship between my daughter and her father.

"Why doesn't he want to see me?" she asked me more than once.

I sighed. "I don't know, baby." I hugged her to my side, squeezing extra tight.

"Doesn't Daddy love me?"

I had no answers for my daughter. I battled my desire to preserve her fragile emotions and the need to tell her the truth. I turned to God, asking for strength to raise my children right.

❧❧❧

The sound of the worship music flowed over me as I walked into Kings Circle. A feeling of rightness filled me, and I raised my hands in praise, surrounded by good friends, many of whom I had known for years.

"Hi, Lynne," the pastor greeted me warmly at the end of the service. "How are you doing with that shoulder?"

I shrugged. "Oh, so-so. I'm scheduled for surgery soon, and I pray that takes care of it."

He nodded and clasped my hand. "We'll be praying for you."

I nodded, genuinely grateful. I appreciated the love and support of my church family, especially my pastor and his wife.

In spite of the troubles in my past, I continued to grow in my relationship with God.

With prayer and God's help, I overcame my addictions to both alcohol and nicotine. I enjoyed going to church and sharing Jesus with everyone I met. I stayed active in my church by teaching Sunday school and volunteering for various church projects. I even started reading the Bible to my mother.

Over the years, learning to trust in God freed me from the fear and guilt of my early years and the burden from my marital challenges.

As I have grown older, my body has grown weaker, but my faith has grown stronger. I've suffered from various debilitating health conditions, the painful loss of my granddaughter and a terminal diagnosis for one of my sons.

Yet in all that, I remained thankful and grateful to God for how far he brought me. I learned to draw strength from knowing that God loves me and that he is on my side, no matter what happens. Every day I woke up was another opportunity to thank God and talk with him.

With that attitude, the only weight I continued to bear was one of undying gratitude and praise.

Thank you, Lord, for setting me free.

Unwavering
The Story of Walter
Written by Alexine Garcia

I found my dad's whiskey hidden in the chicken pen. Whenever I came across those bottles, I'd take a few swigs from one, then put it back where I found it. I was only 10, but I had a taste for the stuff.

That day was no different. I tilted the bottle back, and the liquor burned my throat going down. I put the whiskey back in the box. I giggled to myself and pulled the bottle back out. I poured a good fifth of the bottle in the chickens' water, then put the bottle back. I sat down on a wooden box and watched. It didn't take long before they were flapping around drunk. They wobbled and fell on their faces, and clucks turned into funny noises. I nearly fell off my box laughing. I looked up, and my dad was watching, his face distorted with disgust.

"Boy, you're gonna regret that." He grabbed me by the arm and yanked my pants down. His buckle flew at me, along with a dozen curse words. He walked away still breathing heavily, tired from the work it took to swing his belt with such force.

❧❧❧❧

There are many memories I wish I could forget, including some I cannot personally remember but grew up hearing about. They represent so many dark ink spots on the timeline of my life.

I'm told I was a colicky, crying infant. My mother held and soothed me, but my tears did not let up. One day my dad just couldn't stand my high-pitched wail anymore, so he threw me against the wall. I was only 8 weeks old, and it's a miracle I survived.

This sort of thing was a normal occurrence in our home. Growing up, I had five living siblings and two I would have to meet in heaven. One brother was stillborn, and the other died when he was 8 months old.

Well, I can tell you that it's hard to imagine poor until you have lived in a chicken coop. I remember going to my first day of school barefoot. I didn't own a pair of shoes until I was in the second grade. Tattered clothes, dirty faces and shoeless feet didn't make for attractive features. The kids in my class liked to laugh at my brothers and me, but it was all the same to me.

My first memory of my father was much like the rest of my memories of him. We were traveling through the Southwest to move to a new place. My family moved a lot, actually. We were staying at my aunt's house. My brothers and I never ate candy in our home, so when I came across a cloth bag of sugar, I was elated. I tore a hole in the corner of the sack and sucked out the sweet crystals. My father found me sitting on a pile of mattresses sucking away. He pulled off his large cowboy belt and beat me with the buckle end. I was covered in blood and bruises.

When we lived in Albuquerque, New Mexico, our

property was next to a man who owned beautiful horses. We could tell he really loved those horses because he protected them with an electric fence. I don't remember the offense, but I recall my dad dragging me by the arm across our lot. I begged and pleaded to no end and then was forced to pee on the fence. The electric current was agony. There isn't much physical pain that compares to the shock that flowed through my body that day. At the moment of the first pulse, I was released from the electric grip and ran away with my pants still unzipped around my knees.

When we lived in my uncle's barn in Medford, Oregon, again, I don't remember the wrongdoing, but I do remember hanging from the rafters for several hours, squeezed into a gunnysack.

When I was about 7 years old, my dad taught me a lesson about cigarettes. He used to roll his own cigs and flick the butts out the front door. I found one of the butts on the floor and squatted to inspect it. I picked it up and held it between my fingers and pursed my lips to smoke it. It was an awful experience that only got worse. My father caught me and placed me in a chair. He rolled one after the other and forced me to smoke them. My head pounded with dizziness, and I nearly passed out before he let me quit. By that point, the damage had been done, and I found myself desiring a smoke or two every day.

I don't know why he did these things to us. I would imagine that his heart was black. But my mother's soft, tender heart just about made up for all of my dad's evil intentions. Even though we lived in a coop, a barn or a tent, she used to sweep the dirt floor and then sprinkle water to keep the dust down. And she made sure all of us were fed and content. She loved us dearly, and her sincere smile said it all.

What hurt worse than my dad's belt buckle was watching his fist fly in her face or seeing her collapse to the ground. On several instances, I braced myself for his punch with squinted eyes and rigid muscles only to open my eyes and see that my mother had thrown her body in front of mine to take the blows. That's when my heart would just about collapse with pain.

My brother and I were crying in bed one evening after some beating for some meaningless transgression. We were warm under the blankets in the bed that all us siblings shared. Mom came and sat in a chair next to us with her Bible. She opened the leather cover, like she usually did, and read to us about Jesus from the Book of John: "I have told you all this so that you may have peace in me. Here on earth you will have many trials and sorrows. But take heart, because I have overcome the world." She ran her fingers through my hair and wiped our tears, all the while smiling down on us. She closed her eyes and prayed for us. We bowed our heads and closed our eyes, too.

"Lord, watch over my children, and keep them safe. Heal their little wounded hearts, Father. Your love for them is wide, I know without a doubt."

My mother taught us about praying, God's love, Jesus

and everything else we needed to know about our faith. I believe it was because of her prayers that I even made it in this life. I knew that even though my earthly father was mean and cruel, my father in heaven was a gentle, loving God who cared about me. I imagined that he had tender hands just like my mother.

Despite all this, I still craved my dad's love. I had a parched heart that thirsted for his caring touch. I just wished that he would scoop me up and place me on his knee. But my dad's love was never something to be had, only desired. My yearning hurt worse than all the bruises in the world.

My oldest brother, Donny, used to walk into town to meet up with my dad. He would try and figure out what kind of mood he was in before he could get home. If Dad was in a sour mood, he would scowl at us or cuss up a storm, and that would be the extent of it. If his demeanor was rotten, well, then, that was a different story. Donny would heat up a corked jar filled with water and place it on the counter in warning. When we heard the bubbling noise, we would head for the mountains. We huddled together under the pine trees and open sky and prayed to God for his help. We often cried out in desperation for the anger and abuse to stop.

One day, Donny and I sat at the riverbank and looked out at the afternoon mountains. We were so angry. "I can't bear it much longer," I said.

Donny looked over at me with a determined look on his face. "Let's get rid of the old man."

My head jerked as I looked at him. I searched his eyes for laughter and only found a solemn anger.

"With one of his guns?"

Donny nodded. Our minds were made up. There was nothing but resolve in our hearts until we went home and faced the old man and lost our nerve.

One weekend, some famous evangelist came and set up a huge tent revival. There was music and sermons and the whole bit inside that hot, sweaty tent. On the last day of the revival, the preacher's words spoke right to me. He talked about love, forgiveness and healing. Those were all things I wanted in my life, so I walked right up to the altar when he invited all the people to receive forgiveness for their sins. I held my hands up and prayed with him for Jesus to forgive my sins and come into my heart. A serene peace washed over me. I was only a boy, but I understood that this meant I was "saved." To me, it also meant everything Mom had told me was right: God cared about me, and he forgave my sins.

My brothers and I walked in from school to see my dad hitting my mom. He accused her of sleeping with his brother. He was too senseless to see the good woman he had in front of him. We couldn't stand the sight of her dressing her own cuts and bruises afterward, and so we went to our spot up in the mountains to pray. We asked God to put an end to the madness. We could have filled a bucket with the tears between the lot of us. We were deep in our prayers when I looked up and witnessed something so amazing. I shook my brother, and he opened his eyes, too. My sister gasped at the sight. We all saw what looked like two angels standing a stone's throw away and looking straight at us. A bright sparkling light emitted from their bodies. They had shoulder-length hair and wore white robes. I had never seen anything so bright and shining white in my life. We figured that God sent them to encourage us. That it was a sign that he was working in our lives and answering our prayers.

I read the Bible and prayed with my mother even more after that. I felt like I understood it all. My faith continued to strengthen. My dad's angry hands didn't let up, but I felt God's presence there whenever my brothers and I needed him.

Then the unthinkable happened. The police came and took my father away in the back of a cop car. We found out that he had put his hands on my sister in unspeakable ways. My brothers and I ran out the back of our tent and up to the mountains again. We stopped at the riverbank, and I collapsed onto the soft dark mud. I cried into my palms. I cried so hard that my body shook with each sob.

"How could you let this happen?" Donny yelled at the sky.

"What is the purpose of this, God? Why?" Jared cried.

We prayed until nightfall. We were so mad at God, and our trust in him was shaken.

My father was in jail for almost three years before he was let out on parole. My parents divorced, and my dad moved to New Mexico.

Every weekend, we went to church and attended

Sunday school classes, and I looked to the Bible for solace from the chaos we were living in. One particular Sunday, I listened carefully to the teacher with my brow furrowed with confusion.

"Be perfect, therefore, as your heavenly father is perfect," she said. I think I just about tuned everything else out after she said this.

How the heck am I supposed to be good, much less perfect, like God? If these are his expectations, I want no part in it. Right in that moment, I decided to turn my back on my faith.

I started drinking and continued to smoke. I was a handy kid, and I made a set of keys that could open any locked door in town. The beer warehouse ended up being my favorite spot. I had full access to all the booze I wanted. This behavior carried on into my teens.

❧❧❧

I was out driving drunk without a license and ended up in jail at the age of 16. I was given a choice, and I didn't like either option: live with my dad or join the Navy as soon as I turned 17. I was young, but the military was taking men at the age of 17 with parental consent. I was not ready for such a big decision as joining the Navy, so I chose my dad. As soon as I arrived, the depravity began.

"Put on your coat; we're going out," he said.

After a five-minute drive, we were at a local bar. The place was dimly lit, and a layer of smoke tendrils hung near the ceiling. "I'll have two beers," he told the bartender. I was stunned when he handed me one of the cold bottles.

"Well? Are you going to stare at it or drink it?" He smirked and took a long swig of his beer. I did the same, eyeing him. We played pool and flirted with any girl who came our way.

When we got home to the travel trailer, I lay in my new bed staring at the ceiling and trying to make sense of things. I knew good and well the difference between right and wrong, but we'd had so much fun that night.

Each night after that was pretty much the same. My dad was a completely different man in this atmosphere. He had a hearty laugh that others gathered around. And the women loved him. He charmed their pants off night after night.

If my dad was not at work or asleep, he was drunk or with a woman.

We either went to the bar or Dad's friends came over. He started dating a pretty Mexican woman. She was a good 15 years younger than him, and I dated her younger sister.

My desire for fun battled with my conscience. The faith I thought I had buried turned out to be impossible to uproot. I guess it was so intertwined with who I was.

Dad's family was just like him. His sisters and mother came over to drink and carouse, and no one ever thought any different. I thought being my dad's drinking buddy equated love. I thought perhaps he saw how wrong he'd been all those years. Maybe this was the love I thirsted after for so long.

"Son, you know you don't belong there," my mother pleaded over the phone. I knew she was right. Hearing her talk like that made me feel like I was betraying her. There I was, living with my dad, even after everything he had done.

"I know, Mom. But I don't know what else to do."

"I'm going to send you a bus ticket, and you are going to come home."

A few days later my dad woke up green in the face. He moved around the tiny trailer with a sluggish pace. "You need to get off your fanny, and clean this place up," he said, pointing his finger in my face. This had worked when I was a kid, but I was a man. Or so I thought. I assumed at 16 that he had no right to talk to me like that.

"No."

"What did you say, boy?"

"I said, no."

"You listen to me, kid. When you're big enough to hold your own against me, then you can talk to me like that. But for right now, you'll do as I say."

"Well, I think I'm big enough now," I said, standing up from the couch.

I don't know how much time passed, but I came to and got up off the floor, probably a few hours later.

All that time, I'd clung to his every word. I'd misconstrued the booze and cigarettes for love. I'd thought perhaps this was what I wanted when I was a kid.

But while regaining consciousness on the floor that day, I could see I was completely wrong.

The next morning, I was on a bus going back home. I arrived at the bus stop with no one to pick me up, so I walked eight miles to my mom's place. It was a new scene, but I went right back to the same habits, with my cousin as my drinking buddy.

One evening we sat on the bed of my cousin's truck at the gravel pit drinking quart bottles of beer. We threw our empties at a pile of gravel causing mini-avalanches. We talked about nothing as the beer brought on a drunken stupor.

I wasn't paying much attention to the road behind us when the sheriff pulled up. We both jumped off the truck and hid the current bottle, as neither of us was legally old enough to drink.

"You boys been drinking?"

"No, officer."

"Oh, really? What are those empty bottles doing there?" He pointed to the pile. Being from a small town, the sheriff knew and respected my mom. A lot of people esteemed my mom highly after how she made it through everything. It was well known she was a strong woman.

"Those were already there," my cousin answered.

"Well, they still got foam in them," the sheriff said with a smirk. Both of us looked at him with nothing else to say. "This is what we're going to do, boys. You all are going to get in your truck, and I'm going to follow you to make sure you get home all right."

was a good thing, too. Sammy was swerving all over ι ⸌ road. "You got to drive straight!" I yelled at him.

"I can't see the road right," he said, laughing. "I see two roads. I'm not sure which one to drive on."

"Well, close one eye, and drive on the road you see." We were hooting and hollering, and the sheriff probably thought we were nuts.

We both knew this was not the right way to be living. When I turned 17, my mom signed the consent forms, and we joined the Navy on the buddy system. We were supposed to go to Basic and then get stationed at the same place. But during the Vietnam War, the buddy system was a joke. I didn't see him again for a good while after technical school.

Being in the military felt good. I was always fed, and all my needs were met. Even more so, I had security, something I never felt before in my life. I guess you could say I felt a sense of accomplishment as well. I was trained as a machinist mate and did work in the engine room of Navy ships.

I went on three deployments to Vietnam and visited many foreign ports. At each port, I went on drinking binges to make up for all the lost time while at sea. I thought I was running from God, but I knew all too well God never left my side.

That silent battle continued to wage in my mind. Each side of me fought for control. The drinking and carousing me slowly won real estate. I took my three-day passes and hit as many bars as I could. I often stumbled with blurred vision back aboard the ship with little recollection of the evening's events.

One night I came back in an angry rage. I ended up in the bathroom kicking and punching metal lockers until my knuckles bled. I was not perfect at all. I was not even good, and it bothered me. That Sunday school teacher's words rang in the back of my mind. Even though I turned my back on God, I continued to feel him beckoning me. He invaded my thoughts from time to time. And when the enemy's missiles brought waves of water crashing onto our boats, it was him I called out to. I had a pocket Bible handy that I read in my rack from time to time.

The more I read, the more I realized I was wrong about God's expectations of me. God knew people were going to make mistakes and even reject him. That was the whole reason he sent his son, Jesus. Jesus died because we were not capable of being perfect. That verse that still rang in my head all those years later was talking about growing in perfect maturity after coming to know God. I felt foolish each time I read the Bible. I believed everything it said, but I sure had made a mess of things by that point.

❧❧❧

My life didn't get any better after the war. I married a girl from Hollywood while I was in San Diego, and I never saw her again. Our marriage was annulled, and I married a second time at port in Boston. Wendy gave me two beautiful boys, Tony and Rick, and I adored them both. I was elated to become a father. I was loving with my sons, but I was still a drunk. Wendy ran off with another man, taking our boys. I married a third time and had another son. She also ran off and even got pregnant by another man.

I moved back home. My friend Jim and I started drinking together on the weekends. I was at his house one Friday evening when he said, "Walter, I heard that you once chug-a-lugged a fifth of whiskey."

I laughed and shook my head. He was referring to an event that took place during one of my crazy nights in the Navy. "I sure did, but I'm not proud of it."

"Well, I don't believe you did."

My pride welled up as I continued to shake my head. Jim went inside and came back with a fifth of Seagram's Seven. "I dare you to drink this fifth."

I looked at him, took the drink and tilted my head back as I chugged the whiskey down. When I placed the bottle back down, Jim could hardly sit in his chair, he was laughing so hard. I felt unsteady, and so I knew it was time for me to get going. I rode my motorcycle home through the dark streets. The rest of the night was recounted to me because I never could remember it for myself.

I guess I wasn't quite done with my fun for the night. Once home, I got into my Chrysler Imperial and drove down to the end of 6th Street. I floor-boarded my car all the way down to the other end of town. I then put the car in reverse and sped through town backward, running every single red light. It was a wonder I didn't kill anyone.

By the time several concerned townsfolk had called the police, I'd crossed Caveman Bridge and spun a few brodies in the parking lot of the city park. I suppose I was satisfied with my midnight drive because I parked and got out of my car. I saw a long-haired hippie hanging out. Back then, short-hairs like me and long-hairs like him didn't get along on the account of the ongoing war. So I pulled my hunting knife out of my boot and chased this man through the park. We tumbled to the ground as my hands grasped his neck. I was ready to scalp the man when the cops arrived and tried to pull me off of him. I was pretty strong in my drunken state. It was not until the arrival of Jeff, a buddy of mine who was a police officer, that I was put under control.

He pulled out his Billy club and said, "Walter, I am going to give you two seconds to let go of that man before I knock you in the head."

The next afternoon I sat in a jail cell with a massive headache. *This just isn't right,* I thought to myself. *How could I be so stupid?* At that point, I acknowledged my drinking problem. I wanted badly to change, but doing so seemed nearly impossible.

అఆఆఆ

Despite my crazy lifestyle, I was granted partial custody of Tony and Rick, my sons with Wendy. They made life worth living. We visited my brother Jared often, and each time he had encouragement for me.

"Walter, would you and the boys like to join us for church tonight?" he asked during one visit. I felt shame like bile rise in my throat. It had been so long since I stepped foot in a chapel. I yearned to talk with God and to hear a good, hearty sermon again. Come to think of it, I craved it just like I used to crave a gentle touch from my dad. But at the same time, I felt unworthy of even sitting the seat of my pants down on the wooden pews.

"You know, I think we will join you."

The pastor's words were rich as he read from the Bible and spoke about forgiveness. It was like salve for festering wounds. At the end of the service, the band played, and the pastor invited us to the altar to receive Jesus Christ in our hearts. I had already done this as a young boy, but I knew it was time to return to my roots. I turned back to look at my brother, and he pushed me forward with encouragement. To my surprise, Rick took my hand and walked to the front with me, too. I stood there with my eyes pinched tight and my hands held high, praying, *God, please forgive me. Forgive me for all the years that I turned my back on you. I am so not worthy.*

Jared put his arm around me and gave me a squeeze. "Jesus loves you," he said. It was all too much. I felt relief rush over me like one of those waves of water back on deck. It was all-consuming, and my body collapsed to the ground. I opened my eyes to see Rick and Jared smiling over me. As they helped me to my feet, I rose a different man. I felt it in my gut. The shame was replaced by peace.

Jared was a minister. I visited him now and then and

attended the church sporadically. I often found myself alone with Jared hunched over the pews in deep prayer. He helped me stay connected to God.

Jared lived across the street from his church. I walked over one evening to spend some time with my brother. I slowed down as I approached his house. The most beautiful music I had ever heard came streaming through the screen door. "Music Box Dancer" was playing on the piano. I quietly walked in and watched Denise play as all the wind left my body. Dizzy excitement came over me as her fingers sped through the notes. She was beautiful. I had been married three times before, but this girl was it. I knew right then and there that this was the girl God must have had for me all along; if only I had held out.

Jared stood up from his chair and greeted me at the door. Instead of a cordial hello, I said, "Jared, you gotta set me up on a date with her."

He chuckled and led me to the kitchen.

"No, I don't think this one is for you," he said while serving me a glass of water. It turned out that she was just like a daughter to the pastor. This kind of girl didn't usually go for the likes of me. It was common knowledge that I was a recovering drunk, divorced several times with partial custody of two boys and a daughter that wasn't even mine. Church people loved to see sinners get saved, but it was different when saved sinners wanted to marry a sweet girl like Denise. To my surprise, Denise actually saw something she liked in me. She returned my smile that evening, and we made small talk.

A year later I was sitting on a picnic blanket sharing sandwiches with her. We were at a park across town so that no one we knew would see us. This was how most of our dates took place that year. We were careful not to upset the congregation. We were even more careful about the time we spent together because we wanted to make sure our relationship was right before the Lord.

"You know I'm in love with you, don't you?" I asked her.

She giggled and answered, "I should hope so. I spend nearly all my time hidden away with you."

"Well, I'd be the happiest man alive if you would be my wife."

Her smile quickly turned into a frown. She looked down at her lap and smoothed her skirt. "It's not that I don't want to. I just need to talk this over with my parents. You know that they are wrong about you, but we need their blessing." This was not how I imagined this conversation ending, but I was determined.

We continued to date in secret. Meanwhile, people continued to talk throughout the church. People saw our sideways glances and read between the lines. It was true — for all appearances, I didn't really look like a good fit for Denise.

She was a sweet woman, untarnished by the world's jagged edges. She sang at church and volunteered where she was needed. Everyone knew her to be a nice girl because she was such a people person.

A few weeks later, I was driving her home from a

movie. The sun was setting, sending long orange rays of light through the windshield.

"I need to tell you something, Walter."

"I'm listening."

"I thought about your proposal. Actually, I haven't stopped thinking about it. My answer is yes."

My head snapped in her direction, and I let out a spontaneous hoot. I jerked the car into park right in the middle of the road and got out. I couldn't stop myself from running and dancing around the car. She just sat there and laughed. The orange glow of light radiated over her hair. She looked angelic.

❧❧❧

"No. Not a chance," her father said to me, unwavering.

"Honey, we just don't think that you and Denise are a good match," her mother offered more kindly. Denise and I looked at each other, and I could tell she was holding back tears. She was not one to defy her parents, but this was far from what she wanted. Because of the circumstances, we could not be married in the church of our choice, so we ran off to Tahoe and had a small ceremony with just the two of us. Back at home, the congregation understood that we were determined to be together. They reluctantly threw us a wedding reception. We were too happy to be discouraged by their judgments. In fact, we were so happy with each other that we didn't even have to enjoy their company.

Three years later, I found myself sipping tea and enjoying my father-in-law's company. "You know, son, you really have proven yourself. I couldn't have picked a better husband for my daughter."

I was searching for words, but they stuck in my throat as I fought the emotion threatening to spring from my eyes.

"I want you to know that I consider you like my own son. God has done a good work in you."

My tears poured all over when he reached over and hugged me.

Two years later, we decided to adopt. Our prayers for our baby must have reached God's ears because a few months later we were blessed with Karen, a beautiful little girl from Korea.

We met a caregiver from the adoption agency at the airport to pick up our daughter. I looked down into her eyes, and she was lovely.

"Daddy," she said with a smile. I tell you what, my heart just about slid out of me. Three years later, Priscilla was born. She was our little miracle baby. Denise needed a C-section, and there were complications. A team of doctors worked very hard over the next few hours to sustain Denise's life.

Nine years later, our son Kevin was born. I was blessed to be able to watch his C-section birth. The doctors handed Kevin to me moments after his birth. I looked down at his beautiful pink face and smiled in amazement. I knew I could never lay a fierce hand on something so beautiful. But my love for these children was fierce. I gave them everything. I made sure that my love was not something to be desired, but to be had. I took all my resentment and translated it into a tenderness toward my children.

We celebrated our 25th anniversary by having a wonderful celebration and renewing our wedding vows in a beautiful rose garden.

෨෨෨

Becoming a father was an experience I can't even begin to describe fully. I know that I have three children who don't care to get to know me, and that is the consequence of my own mistakes. I pray for them constantly, and I hope someday they can find a way to forgive me.

I also know I will never be able to display the love my heavenly father has shown me, because his love is so perfect and unwavering. I spent a lot of time running from him, but I believe he stayed right by my side through it all, because he is not a God who gives up on us.

Denise and I began attending Kings Circle Assembly of God Church every Sunday, and it became like a second home to us. The people are not just church members, but family. From the moment we first arrived, we were always received as friends.

I've always treasured the memory of that day Denise sat and laughed as I danced around the car. We were an unlikely couple by society's standard. But it was a good thing for me that neither God nor Denise judged based on outward appearances. She is my anchor. She has been by my side and helped me to remain faithful and centered on Christ.

She also gave me the gift of fatherhood, and for that, I could never be thankful enough.

Into the Light
The Story of Crystal
Written by Rosemarie Fitzsimmons

"That's it, amigos, we're shutting down early." Mike, my boss, started tossing glasses in a plastic bin and wiping down the bar. "Drive safe now. It's really starting to pile up out there."

Mike disappeared into his office behind the bar, and the handful of regulars grumbled and shuffled into their coats. I un-tucked the towel from my apron and wiped clear a circle in the fogged window so I could peer out. My VW Bug was already entombed by more than a foot of snow.

Great. I won't be sleeping there tonight. I'd been living out of my car for at least a week.

Bear, the last customer to leave, staggered to the door where I waited with the key to lock up behind him. He'd been at the bar most of the day, drinking orange juice and crème de menthe to slow the pace of his buzz. *Yum, like toothpaste and beer.* Bear rarely spoke to me, aside from requesting a refill. But he slid me a coy, yellow smile as he steadied himself at the door, fumbling through his pockets for his car keys.

"Ya need sum-place ta stay?"

No, no, no! Not if you were the last man on earth.

There were no shelters nearby, and I had no family in

the area, no friends. I looked with revulsion at his bloodshot eyes and leering grin.

And I nodded.

We climbed into his truck and drove into the storm. I said nothing, but stared through the wipers at the road, thinking about the baby inside me. I considered it somewhat ironic that I'd sworn off sleeping with men for the baby's sake, and yet, here I was.

Can it get any worse?

Bear's rundown shack was a mile or so away. When he opened the door, I nearly gagged from the pungent smell of filth and garbage. Dirty dishes and cans were stacked everywhere. Two grimy boys, about 10 and 12 years old, sat quietly on a rickety bed in the shadows. I didn't even know he had kids since he was at the bar most nights. I was repulsed. He pointed me to the other bed; his eyes gleamed.

By some incredible stroke of luck, Bear was too drunk to do anything other than fondle me. But he managed to stay awake long into the night, cursing and fondling while I stared at the dirty darkness overhead. I felt ashamed, degraded and hopeless. Silent tears slipped down my face as I remembered the girl I'd been four short years before — a singer and model in complete control of her future, or so I'd thought.

It had been a long time since I'd sung anything.

I had a sunny but strict childhood. My mother had been in her mid-30s when I was born, and my dad was about 10 years older than her. They were both Christians, and they raised me as best they knew how and prayed for me often.

Mom was like other women of her era — Dad wore the pants, and she went along.

Dad had lost his mother when he was 4 years old and was raised by my aunts and under the watchful eye of a grandmother who preached for a Methodist church. He raised us five kids (I had two half-brothers on my mom's side, a half-sister on my dad's and a full sister who is seven years older) as he'd been raised — no nonsense. He was a disciplinarian.

Like other men of his era, my father took his role as the leader of the house seriously. When I was young, he beat me repeatedly for wetting the bed because he thought I was lazy. He didn't stop until one night when I fell asleep on his lap and the unthinkable happened. He must have realized I really couldn't help it, no matter how much he beat me. Still, his discipline left me feeling rejected. Although he loved me, I never felt good enough or perfect enough in his eyes. It made me a perfectionist in many areas, trying to make myself someone of value. I did well in school, I didn't get in trouble and I succeeded in most endeavors.

At school, though, I was a bit of a loner. I had trouble keeping friends. I'd have them for a few days and then they'd start to disappear. Someone even tried to beat me up in the third grade, but I didn't know why. I later understood that I had a high opinion of myself and that I often criticized others, not realizing my words might have hurt them. I was also a bit of a chatterbox, and I sang *all* the time.

We moved from Iowa to Prescott Valley, Arizona, the summer before my fourth grade year, then to the Phoenix area two years later and finally to Scottsdale, where I stayed through high school. In Scottsdale, I learned to cuss and push back. It seemed like everyone else cursed, and I wanted to fit in.

๛๛๛

"I think I'm going to be a model." My friend Sara pushed her lunch tray aside and pulled a compact from her purse. She dabbed some powder on her blemish-free nose, nodded at her reflection and then snapped the compact closed. "Did you know there are schools just for modeling?"

I liked Sara. She was one of the reasons I enjoyed my new school.

"Modeling. That sounds like fun. Maybe I will, too." I didn't need a compact to know it wasn't likely. I was about 105 pounds, and some people said I was pretty. But in my eyes, the only thing about me that drew people's attention away from my naturally curly, circus-clown hair was my out-of-proportion nose. Still, a girl could dream.

"Aren't models kind of tall?" I tried to picture my gangly self lumbering down a catwalk.

"You! A model! That's a laugh!" Chris Carter dropped with a thud into the chair next to mine, still chewing a bite of chicken sandwich. He was one of the few reasons I *didn't* like my new school. My parents had enrolled me there after some kids beat me up in public school. They certainly couldn't afford it, but Mom worked in the front office so I'd been accepted on scholarship. Privileged folk, like the Carters, didn't think much of people on scholarship.

"What makes you think you could ever be a model?" He meant me, but glanced at Sara, who looked down at the table. "Now, Sara, here, she's a fox. She could be on any magazine cover in the world. But you ..."

He leaned in so close I could smell the yeast from his sandwich bread.

"You'll never, *ever* be a model. You're so ugly, nobody could possibly want you."

His words stung, and they reaffirmed my dim view of myself. I'd never be desirable.

Who could want me, indeed?

సౌసౌసౌ

I started smoking marijuana the summer before I entered ninth grade. Even though I knew everyone at our church's new private school, many of the students were from well-off families, and I still felt as if I didn't fit in. I developed a mantra that enabled me to shut out the fear of potential consequences in favor of acceptance: "I'll try anything once."

First pot, then drinking, then boys. Once never turned out to be enough.

My career plan during my high school years had been to go to Europe and study opera. I sang well, and music was a huge part of my life.

At a voice recital, I met Greyson, a student at Arizona State University. We dated about two years. He was a good guy, and I'm sure he turned out to be a good man, but I didn't take our relationship seriously, even after we became intimate. "You're pretty adventurous," Greyson said.

Adventurous. I liked the label. This guy in my English class named Brian liked it, too. I was still dating Greyson, and I'd never cheated on him, but ... *I'll try anything once.*

At first I thought everything was fine because I was keeping my grades up and, more importantly, I was having fun. In reality, we were flirting with danger and self-destruction.

I made one I'll-try-anything concession after another. Brian and I skipped school a lot, spending our days smoking pot, listening to rock and roll in a dark room with a black light on and having sex. I did all my class work at the last minute. I was fairly smart, so I could get away with not studying. Brian simply worked hard when we weren't together. I left Greyson behind.

I evened the score with Chris Carter when the Ford Modeling Agency selected my photo from among thousands as one of their top-200 faces in the nation. I started taking local modeling jobs. Swimwear? Lingerie? Sure. *Just this once.*

I knew I was overexposed; my conscience nagged at me. But I ignored it and told myself I could laugh all the way to the bank. Besides, I had my pick of men at the agency — handsome men. I was naïve enough to think their admiring looks were not lust but desire, and as *everyone knows,* one reciprocates desire by offering sex. Alcohol and drugs (I'd graduated to cocaine) flowed freely. I felt powerful and in control. Knowing Brian had no clue what I was up to only increased my feeling of power.

When my parents moved to Reno, Nevada, I chose to stay behind. Brian and I found an apartment, and I told Mom and Dad we were just roommates. At first it was fun, but aside from our self-destructive lifestyles, we had little in common. The relationship fizzled, and Brian left to join the Army. For whatever reason, he came back and proposed to me. I don't know why I married him. Yet I did believe I loved him at the time.

I left the modeling behind and moved to Fort Carson, Colorado, where Brian was stationed. In my mind, I would be the perfect wife and keep the perfect house. Once I even cleaned the waxed-over linoleum in our apartment using a toothpick to get every bit of dirt out of the cracks in the floor. However, we continued our high school behavior, hosting wild parties and overindulging in alcohol and all sorts of drugs. I'm surprised he didn't get caught in a drug test.

Such a weak foundation couldn't support us for long, and we divorced after about 18 months. I got a job serving cocktails at a trendy place and moved into a house with a couple of the bartenders. When the bartenders moved away, I couch surfed and ended up sleeping with a series of boyfriends. I didn't sleep with them to hurt them — I cared about them. I just thought it was what you did. Deep down, my conscience screamed at me, but I honestly believed a man's desire was the opposite of rejection. I *so* desperately needed not to feel rejected.

This behavior continued until I turned 22, at which time I became pregnant. I swore I'd clean up my act.

No more men.

I'd been living out of my car and searching for an apartment to rent when the blizzard hit. That long night in Bear's shack was the most humiliating experience of my life, and I left feeling as if I couldn't stoop any lower.

And yet I did.

❧❧❧

"Crystal, you're next." The woman looked at me briefly, then wrote something on her clipboard.

It took all my strength to stand and walk toward her. My heart pounded so hard I could barely breathe.

This is wrong. You can't really be here.

But, for the millionth time, I looked at my life, and I knew I must. I was ill-prepared to be a mother. I was doing 12 to 15 shooters a night, smoking pot, snorting coke. The baby could have all sorts of defects.

I just can't do that to a child. This is the humane thing to do, right? I have no choice.

The woman led me to a small room and asked a few questions. I so desperately wanted her to touch my hand. Pat my shoulder. Look at me. But she was all business. She did not ask why. She did not ask if I was sure. I was just "next."

I walked out of the clinic a few hours later, no longer pregnant. I felt sick with self-loathing. My conscience nagged at me, *Why did I do this?*

Mortified, embarrassed and angry with myself that I got pregnant in the first place, I'd never felt such despair.

That night, I was unpacking boxes in my new apartment when I pulled out a plaque and unwrapped the newspaper packed around it.

I hadn't seen this item in a long while. I'd bought it for my parents but had never given it to them. The book-shaped board was divided down the middle, with a question on one side that read, "I asked Jesus, 'How much do you love me?'"

On the other side was the answer: "Jesus said, 'This much.' Then he stretched out his arms and died."

My heart broke. I just sat there, staring at the plaque and sobbing. I realized I no longer cared about acceptance. My heart yearned for safety and stability. I thought of my parents' home and their relationship with God, and I felt drawn to the hope I might find with them.

I packed back up and turned toward California, where they were living. I didn't know at the time how long and dark the road ahead would be. I only knew I saw a glimmer of light, and I wanted it.

రావాలా

I started over in California, still broken but full of hope. It wasn't long before I met Benny at a local racquetball club. He was much older than I. He had a home, a construction business and kind eyes. I could talk to him. He knew I was struggling financially, and I told him I needed to go to the dentist, so when he asked me to help him with a construction project in Texas in return for some dental work, I agreed.

Benny went to a Catholic church, and I felt comfortable talking to him. During the long drive to Texas, we had real conversations, and I started to like him. We even talked about faith.

"I just feel out of control, Benny." I'd never told anyone about my life before. It made my heart feel lighter somehow to confide in him. "My thoughts stray all the time, and I keep doing stupid things."

"You just have to make God your partner one minute at a time." He smiled at me with genuine affection. "Before you know it, it's one hour at a time, and then day by day."

It made sense. I said a silent prayer for God's forgiveness, which I repeated many times after that day.

On the return trip, Benny changed the subject.

"You know, you're safe with me. I won't hurt you." He put his hand on mine. "Now that I've gotten to know you, I don't think I want to live without you."

Safety, security. *Was Benny the answer?*

He didn't do drugs. He worked hard. He seemed safe.

"I feel the same way, Benny."

Pleased, he said, "Well, now, why don't we marry ourselves right here in the truck?"

He pulled over, and we watched the sun set, and we vowed to be faithful to each other before God. When we got back, we drove over to my parents' house and told them our news. They looked a bit dumbfounded, but what could they do?

Benny was convinced our relationship honored God, and he had no intention of marrying me legally. For a while, he was all I needed. He was a construction worker and had literally built his own business, so I wanted for nothing. Despite Benny's age, he acted young. My health and figure improved significantly from regular racquetball workouts, waterskiing and swimming. Benny and I lived together for five years. I did what I knew to cultivate a relationship with God, going to church with Benny and sometimes to my parents' church as well.

But when I met someone new, I just left.

෴෴෴

I'd decided to enroll at Butte Community College to become a physical therapist. On the first day of class, the instructor asked us to share textbooks. I shared with Tom. We were soon in a study group together. Eventually we started going out for drinks after class.

One night while we were out, he told me his story. He said that he was leaving his wife and listed the reasons he felt justified in doing so. He wanted to get into nursing school because he needed a job that would pay child support for four kids. I told him my story. He put down his beer and, after a long dramatic pause, pledged his love to me.

"Benny's a fool not to make it legal." Tom's baby-blue eyes looked puppy-dog loyal. "You're definitely worth marrying. If you were mine, I'd put you on a pedestal, and you'd never be dishonored again. We would go to church together and raise a Christian family."

I was so naïve, I fell right into his trap. I left Benny for Tom and married him the moment the ink dried on his divorce papers.

Shame and self-loathing came rushing back. I thought I'd had it all together. I thought I'd committed to Benny for a lifetime. I thought I'd found a normal life. But from what I could see, I was as out of control as ever.

We moved in with Tom's parents and started a business. I was never comfortable there, particularly because his mother didn't seem to like me. I tried to stay out of her way, using the appliances when she was out and helping where I could.

We'd only been married a few months when I met another side of Tom's personality.

"Oh, Crystal, this is my favorite movie! Come watch it with me." Tom tried to grab my arm as I passed behind the couch.

"Sure. Just let me grab the clothes from the dryer." I was back with the full laundry basket in minutes. I stood behind him and began sorting socks.

"Sit down, you're missing it." He sounded like a petulant 5 year old.

"I can watch it from here, babe. I really need to get these folded."

"Dammit!"

Tom jumped up and gave me an ice-cold glare before storming outside, slamming the door behind him. I felt numb and frightened.

What did I do?

He didn't return until the following day. I learned later that he'd spent the night in the car. He said he felt disrespected and angry that I couldn't understand how important the movie was to him.

After that day, it became clear that Tom was an alcoholic. He was an angry drunk. I never knew what would set him off, spewing curses and ranting. There was no peace. When we fought, more often than not he would say, "If you want a divorce, just go get the papers, and I will sign them, but I will never leave you."

The business failed, so we headed north to Oregon where Tom's extended family lived. We found work and eventually settled in Corvallis. Tom continued to drink, a lot, and he collected comics, even when we didn't have enough money for the basics. He viewed pornography openly, insisting that he had no lust, but that he was only admiring the women's beauty. He claimed I was the sexiest woman he had ever seen. To me, it still felt like rejection.

There was a lot of good about Tom. He had an over-the-top genius IQ. He was hysterically funny, smart, popular, charismatic and, right or wrong, he passionately believed in whatever he was saying. He also knew he was broken. His parents had raised him in a religion that taught salvation was all about what you did and that only a limited number of people were going to make it to heaven. Tom had a problem with that, so he spent time searching for a better answer, at one point deciding he was an atheist. Then he was lured into a pagan-like cult, only to leave in frustration because of their rituals and practices.

"They're just as religious as Christians!" He eventually stopped searching.

I was so unhappy during those times. I started to remember the peace I'd felt going to church with Benny. I decided to look for a church in Corvallis. Tom said I could look, but he wouldn't go with me.

The second week, I struck gold when I found a little church. I walked in guarded and scared, but it felt like home. The people there were quite nice, and they accepted me right away. I bounded through the front door that afternoon, elated. I thought Tom would be thrilled for me, but he wasn't. He acted as though I was cheating on him — *with God?* I didn't get it. I was devastated. *Didn't he want what was best for me?* I kept going back, however, leaving him an open invitation, hoping he would change his mind.

That church touched my heart. At first, I felt as if I had to look the part and hide all of my brokenness, but as the weeks passed, I learned how to let Jesus change my heart, little by little. The people there prayed for and encouraged me. I was feeling more and more light inside me, decision by decision, prayer by prayer.

One unexpected influence that really changed me and helped me heal was a man at the church named Dale. He was there every Sunday, helping with the sound, ushering and filling in wherever he saw a need.

He sat near me in church, and during the time for greeting each other, he almost always hugged me and said something encouraging. His hugs felt different — clean. After all the men I had known, I could pick up on lust as if it had its own scent. Dale showed none.

Despite all the stress, Tom and I wanted a child and were thrilled to learn I was pregnant. Early on, though, I started bleeding and cramping, and we learned I had an ectopic pregnancy, which meant it was outside the uterus. I lost the child, as well as one of my fallopian tubes. I figured either I wouldn't or couldn't bear children.

I stopped drinking (I'd quit doing drugs when I met Benny). I didn't make a big deal out of it, but I'd cut way down and just wasn't enjoying alcohol anymore. However, when I told Tom, he became angry, as if he was losing his drinking buddy.

Between his drinking and volatile outbursts, he'd still confess an undying love for me, but I was miserable at home and couldn't say with any certainty that I loved him.

Less than a year later, I was staring at a doctor in shock as I learned I was pregnant again. Elated beyond words, I could only pray. "Wow, God. Thank you! I want you to know, if I *never* have a child, I will be content. The odds against this were huge, yet here I am. I trust you and whatever you have planned."

I went into labor six weeks early. At the hospital, the staff admitted me and pumped me full of drugs to stop the contractions. Tom offered to spend the night, but I sent him home to be with his boys. Admittedly, I was under the influence of some powerful muscle relaxants, but what happened next, well, nobody will ever convince me it didn't happen.

❧❧❧❧

"I'm so afraid, God. Please let this baby live."

My hospital room was dark, except for what hallway light came in through the door, which stood slightly ajar. I felt so alone.

I began to sing quietly. "Jesus loves me, this I know, for the Bible tells me so. Little ones to him belong. They are weak, but he is strong. Yes, Jesus loves me ..."

To my amazement, a watery, oval hole seemed to form on the wall across the room, like a portal in some weird time-travel scene. Then I saw Jesus there, just looking at me, smiling.

His peace filled the room, changing the atmosphere around me. I felt everything that was dark — all fear, all trauma, all sadness — just leave. I knew, even without asking, that darkness couldn't stay in his presence.

"Lord. What do you want to do?" I was prepared to do whatever he asked.

He just smiled and lingered a bit. I watched him until the vision faded; his peace stayed behind, and I fell fast asleep. The peace I felt never left me. I'd need it in the weeks and months to come.

The contractions stopped, and I was able to go home. However, my baby was not out of danger. On the day of my scheduled delivery, something went wrong. His little heart faltered, and I was quickly rushed into the ER for an emergency C-section.

When Ian was born, I didn't even get to hold him before they whisked him away.

How can we bond if I don't hold him? I'd heard stories of how important that first moment was. Tom came into the recovery room and tenderly told me that Ian was being transported to Portland and that he might not live. I had faith that he would make it. I was worried, but I clung to the memory of that peaceful night with Jesus for strength.

Tom and I raced to Portland, where we found Ian in an open layette with a heat light above him; he was full of tubes and wires. I still couldn't pick him up. I can't describe the love I felt for my little boy. Weighed down with sadness, I began to sing "Jesus Loves Me." Ian recognized my voice, and his eyes turned in my direction. Elation filled my heart as I realized, *We already bonded, before he was born.*

In the coming years, Ian would go through open-heart surgery, cranial and facial reconstruction and receive a shunt in his brain, as well as a host of other operations, some requiring skin and bone grafts. One of the doctors who presented his initial assessment told us that our son would likely never eat or breathe without life support.

When Ian was 10 days old, I sat at his layette with tears in my eyes.

"I've never held my son," I said to the nurse on duty.

"Oh, we can't have that," she said. She got me a rocker and laid him in my arms on his fleece, tubes, wires and all. My heart nearly burst with joy. Ian hooked his feeding tube with his tiny hand and pulled it out.

"Well, then." The nurse seemed unfazed. "We may as well try giving him a bottle before we replace the tube." She gave me a small bottle of formula. Ian gulped and gasped, but he drank the milk.

That Sunday, I attended a nearby church. The woman who drove me there told the Sunday school group about Ian and asked if they'd pray. Everyone held hands and prayed for us. Afterward, a man who'd prayed said he'd seen a vision of God's hand sewing up Ian's heart. I thought, *I don't have enough faith for this.*

Then a somewhat timid lady came up to me and said, "I believe God wants you to know that you don't have to have a lot of faith, only a tiny amount."

How did she know what I was thinking?

Ian came home when he was a month old and had heart surgery less than three months later. His life has been fraught with medical issues, but he has turned out to be one of the most amazing, upbeat, positive gifts of a son anyone could ask for. His heart is perfect now. Even with surgery, I believe this outcome was nothing short of a miracle. Ian makes an impact on everyone he meets and strives to make strangers feel welcome. His infectious grin and joyful, "Hi, I'm Ian!" breaks down many walls and barriers not otherwise penetrable.

And, as if God wanted to be sure I knew how much he wanted to bless me, our daughter Joy came several years after Ian, as an unexpected gift. She brought sunshine and joy into our home. She had a difficult time adjusting to Ian's health requirements, as they came first. Our lifestyle was challenging for the entire family.

I continued to attend church and study the Bible, and I began to see less of myself and more of the world around me. Raising Ian meant spending a lot of time in children's hospitals. I saw tiny sick infants, many wrapped in special plastic film to protect their fragile skin. Pictures of children taken progressively through their battles began to move my heart. For the first time, I accepted that I had taken a life when I had that abortion, and I believed there must have been a soul inside of that baby. As I was processing all of this, I found a book at Options Pregnancy Center in Corvallis written by another woman who had an abortion and who had come to the same conclusion. I experienced deep inner healing through reading that book and praying for my child and for forgiveness.

One evening I went to a ladies prayer meeting,

desperate for a break and to be refreshed. During the program, the speaker began praying for individuals in the audience. She looked right at me and said, "God wants to give you the deepest desire of your heart. What is it?"

I thought about my life. Many aspects needing fixing, but there was one desire burning above all in my heart. "I want a healthy, godly home."

I closed my eyes while she prayed, and I pictured a beautiful old wooden jewelry box lined in velvet. Inside were antique platinum and diamond heirloom pins. When I opened my eyes, I knew that these pieces represented family heritage, passed from generation to generation. This picture became my prayer. I also imagined a yellow house in a safe neighborhood, with a fenced yard, fruit trees and a large garden. Inside lived a godly family and a couple of dogs. It was my picture of heaven on earth. In my heart, I said, *Okay, God, I expect to receive this.*

That day when I went home, nothing had changed, but I had acquired an ability to love my husband the way I once had, even though he was getting sicker, more volatile and harder to live with by the day. I realized over time that I was changing, despite my circumstances.

❦❦❦

Tom tried to hide his deteriorating health from me. On top of alcohol-related issues, the arthritis in his hip was worsening. He downed ibuprofen like candy and drank to kill the pain in his hip, as well as his heart. He continued to say he didn't believe in organized religion. The one time he joined me and the boys at church, he got mad at me over something little, stormed out and walked the several miles home. He treated me with hatred and distain most of the time after that.

The most significant change in Tom's personality occurred in 2001, when the World Trade Center was destroyed by terrorists. We were all in shock, but Tom's reaction went deeper. He wouldn't let the kids play in the yard alone even for a second. He wouldn't let us answer the door unarmed (fearing the person could be a jihadist) and wouldn't let the kids attend public school.

He did, however, resume his search for God. At one point, Tom said he'd come to know the Lord, but when he learned the Lord wanted Tom to trust him with his will, Tom said, "I will never give up my will!"

After a battle, Tom agreed to be seen at the Roseburg VA clinic. One of his legs had swollen up like a tree trunk, his hip was bad and his liver was well on its way to being shot. The doctor told him livers can renew themselves and that he had a chance, but he'd have to quit drinking. He cut down for about two weeks. I prayed every day for the Lord to heal him. I didn't want to lose him.

By 2005, I'd been homeschooling, and my children had no friends. I wanted them to interact with other children, but I also worked part time. So I started them in a children's program at Kings Circle Assembly of God that met on Wednesday nights. I met a new friend named David there, teaching the youth. I began to help out, and we became real friends. It was liberating to have a healthy, honest friendship with a man.

One afternoon, I was painting a room and listening to music when I started to pray. "Lord, I've been praying for Tom all these years. I don't even know if I am supposed to anymore. I am so confused and tired. I give up, Lord. You just do what is best with him."

Two days later, Tom called my name from his room. I raced in and found him on the floor.

"Help me up! I'm too weak!"

I couldn't lift him. Soon blood started coming out of his mouth. I called for an ambulance and then called a friend to pick up the kids. Tom never left the hospital. I stayed with him until the heart monitor flat-lined a few days later. Shortly before he passed, something wonderful happened. He was in and out of consciousness by then, but I felt like the Lord was doing something. All of that junk he was carrying around seemed to be leaving — the fear, the hatred, the heaviness was replaced with a sense of contentment that I hadn't seen in him before. I believed Tom finally made his peace with God, and I was grateful that the Lord let me witness this incredible gift.

My oldest stepson and his wife were with me when we told the little ones Daddy had died. Ian went to the bathroom, sickened by the news. Joy just sobbed. We asked the kids if they had any questions. Ian said, "Since I am the man of the house, does that mean that I can cuss now?"

The people at Kings Circle were so compassionate to

us. Right before the funeral, Ian had an opportunity to go to a Royal Rangers campout (the church's program for young boys). Royal Rangers meant so much to Ian; one of his older half-brothers took him to the event so he wouldn't miss it. Many people reached out to us. I am still grateful for their love and kindness. Joy was angry that he died. She was mad at God for not saving her daddy.

I was stunned. I remembered the jewelry box and cried out, "God, I was sure that was you who gave me the picture. Now that he is gone, does it still have meaning?" I sensed a very strong YES.

But how could it? This doesn't make sense.

৵৵৵

We started our new life after Tom passed. We should have been dirt poor, just scraping by, but somehow, there was never an unpaid bill. People covered our backs, and real financial provision came in whenever we needed it. Kings Circle became our church.

I thought that God might have another husband for me one day. I daydreamed about who he'd be. Certainly, someone who loved Jesus more than anything, even me, but also an outdoorsman, who was gentle but strong, who laughed easily, but didn't have a dirty sense of humor. He would love me just as I was, despite my past. He would have to love my kids and be a real dad, too. He would have the means to support us as well.

A little more than a year after Tom's death, I ran into

David again. He had suffered a bitter loss at about the same time as our family did. We resumed our friendship, and it blossomed into more, quickly. We both had an inner peace that we were meant to marry, and on May 1, he proposed to me. We went through premarital counseling and married the following October with our pastor's blessing.

Our marriage was healthy. From the time we started dating, David was *never* harsh or unkind to me. Our family bonded, and David took on the role of a true father. The kids loved him as their dad in return. In fact, David brought a stable, loving presence into Joy's life that helped her make peace with her father's passing. Beyond this, I saw how God gave me all of the things I prayed for (well, my house is not yellow), but none of it could compare to the healthy home, the heritage I wanted to pass down to my children. Our personal life has a light and purity about it that once didn't seem possible. God did answer my prayer and gave me my heart's deepest desire.

Kings Circle Assembly of God became our home church, and we remained very active there. We appreciated how the children's program and youth group impacted our kids and grandkids. More importantly, we admired the church's outreach program, which served those in need through helping shelter families, single moms, missionary efforts and by demonstrating many other avenues of selflessness. The more we got to know and build relationships with people there, the richer our lives became.

❧❧❧

"Hi, I'm Ian. Welcome to Kings Church!" My son extended his hand to an awkward-looking young man and pumped heartily. The awkwardness began to dissipate, and the young man grinned.

"Hi, I'm Nate. Glad to meet you, Ian."

The two new friends walked into the sanctuary, Ian pausing to introduce Nate to people along the way. Nate was quickly swallowed up by the loving crowd.

I turned to David, who looked at me with genuine love, and took the arm he offered. A beam of sun streaked into the room, creating a walkway before us. We stepped onto it and entered the sanctuary, filled with joy and eager to sing praises to our Lord.

A Guy, a Girl and a Parked Van
The Story of Greg
Written by Lisa Bradshaw

"I need your help, Kelly," I told my friend, calling her late one night on the way home from a party. "I need to borrow your jack. I hit a curb and got a flat tire."

"I don't think I have a jack."

"You definitely have a jack. Your car is brand new."

"I'm not sure I do," she continued.

I quickly grew frustrated with Kelly and hung up the phone when I saw a police car driving by.

He'll have a jack!

I waved him down and asked him if I could use his jack after telling him about hitting the curb.

"I'll give my buddy a call," he said. "He's got a jack."

"Oh, thanks. Thanks a lot." I was so drunk it hadn't occurred to me that he was calling for a field sobriety officer to come check me out and haul me off to jail if I failed the test. The officer gave me the sobriety test. I failed miserably and had to spend the rest of the night in jail.

"My girlfriend left me," I cried to the booking officer. "She's pregnant with my baby and won't talk to me." I was pouring my heart out to him, hoping he could see I was just a guy in a bad place.

"Listen, don't let this arrest ruin your life," he advised me. "I've seen this happen to a lot of good people. You can recover from it. Just turn your life around from this point on." A drunk guy crying about losing his pregnant girlfriend probably wasn't anything new to him, but going through it was definitely new to me.

Despite wanting to make a change in my life, getting a DUI wouldn't help me in my efforts to convince Mary and her family to give me another chance.

❧❧❧

My dad was an athletic, strong and capable man. He won awards in high school and lettered in several sports. He was a track and field star and an amateur boxer. He was the epitome of good health, so being diagnosed with Parkinson's disease at the age of 25 changed everything. My mom soon left my dad, my sister and me. The responsibility of caring for two young children and a husband with a debilitating disease probably frightened and overwhelmed my mother.

My dad was loving, strict, uncompromising and incredibly supportive. He needed help shaving and sometimes cooking dinner, but he made good use of his medication's two-hour reprieve from the stiffness and tremors — that's when he would exercise and make us dinner. The rest of the time he went through periods of being utterly frozen or completely unable to control his movements.

My dad always said there would be a cure for Parkinson's disease. Never once did he act as if the disease was a death sentence. To us, he made it seem like it was a hiccup on the way to healthiness, and I admired him for his ongoing efforts and determination.

For as much as he tried to remain positive and continued to be an outstanding father, he struggled being in public after his diagnosis. Uncontrollable shaking caused by the disease and his experimental medication made it difficult for him to face people who once knew him for his athleticism. It eventually broke him down so much that he became agoraphobic — he wouldn't leave the house.

My dad's parents and Aunt Marion and Uncle Greg helped raise my sister Cindy and me. I was actually named after my uncle. When my dad stopped leaving the house, my sister and I would shop at the local convenience store for groceries in between my grandma's more extensive shopping for us.

We lived next to my grandparents and my aunt and uncle until I was 5. Our backyards were connected, so we'd just go from one house to the next. When we later moved out to the country, we still saw them on a regular basis and spent the night with my grandparents every Friday night. Having extended family close by was a huge help to my dad and a gift to us.

We saw our mom on holidays and some weekends throughout our childhood. There were times when she was supposed to show up for visits but didn't. When we were younger, it felt like work visiting her, but she tried to be a good mom when she was with us. She remarried when I was 8, but my sister and I always felt most comfortable with my dad and his extended family.

తతతత

"If I ever catch or hear about any of my grandkids doing drugs, I'm going to come up behind them and hit them on the head with a frying pan," my grandpa told me when I was a teenager. I had no doubt he would do exactly that, so I never touched drugs, and I didn't let him know when I started casually drinking at 14.

About this time, Aunt Marion died. She was much older than my grandma and had helped raise her when they were young. It was my first experience with death, and watching my grandma struggle with the loss of her sister was difficult to see.

When I was 18, my dad had a highly experimental surgery and was one of the first people to have brain stimulators placed deep inside his brain. The surgeons drilled holes into his skull and pushed wires down into the speech center in the middle of his brain. The wires were secured under his skin and ran down the side of his skull to battery packs on his upper left shoulder and his lower right abdomen.

My grandpa called me at work a few days after my dad's surgery.

"Your dad is in real trouble. You need to get up here right now."

It was the first time I had ever heard fear in my grandpa's voice. I got in my car and drove as fast as I could to the hospital.

"Get away from me!" my dad yelled, wailing and fighting off the army of medical staff trying to restrain him. He thought he was being abducted by aliens and was trying to pull the wires from his head. He had lifted weights every day of his life for 20 years and was incredibly strong and difficult to control, so the nurses had to start restraining him when he slept and waking him slowly. They would then remove the restraints once he had his wits about him.

No one knew what to expect because it was such an experimental procedure, but we didn't expect him to act like a 12-year-old boy. He would sit on his hospital bed with his arms coiled around his knees watching television and carried on conversations using the dialogue and maturity of a young kid. We were so relieved once he got through the initial brain trauma of the surgery and started acting normal again. We were even more thrilled to discover the procedure had regressed his disease by 15 years. No one knew how long the benefits would last, but we were hopeful the improvements would be permanent.

While the surgery helped mask a lot of his symptoms, it didn't cure the disease, so he still had problems with balance, and he started stuttering. It was fascinating because when he turned the deep brain stimulators off, he could speak perfectly, but he couldn't move. The stimulators masked his symptoms as long as they were turned on, but they impeded his speech, so he couldn't have full use of his body and his speech at the same time.

This became our new normal, and we all adapted to it, still believing that there would be a cure for Parkinson's disease in our future. In the meantime, for the first time in years, my dad started feeling comfortable leaving the house. Dad started doing the grocery shopping for Uncle Greg the way Aunt Marion had done for us. This made it all the more painful for my dad when my family suffered another loss and Uncle Greg died a couple years after Aunt Marion.

❧❧❧

Dad wasn't a man who wore his heart on his sleeve, but we were extremely close. He was my best friend. When I decided to move in with my girlfriend, Cara, he cried.

I liked living with my dad. I only moved out because Cara needed the financial help after she was kicked out of her house. I was 21 and perfectly happy living at my dad's house, but I felt like I was doing the right thing at the time, and he understood.

I started drinking more heavily. All I did was work and drink. I didn't let my dad or grandpa know just how bad it was and would only have a casual beer with my dad when watching a football game or hanging out together after I moved in with Cara.

Cara and I broke up about three years later but still hung out sometimes with our mutual friends. We got along fine until a camping trip with a group of people changed everything.

❧❧❧

"My friend is arriving the last day of camp," Cara's friend Joanie kept telling us. "She's the coolest girl you're ever going to meet." She went on and on about this friend of hers, but Joanie was so strange that I didn't think much of anyone she might be bringing along.

On the last night of the camping trip, in walked her friend. Not only was Mary absolutely beautiful, but she was also carrying a bunch of beer. She made a memorable entrance. Despite my smelling like my circumstances — no shower and the stench of beer — we soon hit it off and ended up hooking up that night.

The next morning proved awkward. Cara wasn't too happy that I had hooked up with someone with her around, and no one was too happy that I had made out with a married woman. I knew she was married, but I didn't care, and Mary didn't seem to mind, either. It didn't occur to me then that she might have cheated on her husband many times, that I might not be anyone special to her. I was completely taken by her from the moment we met.

On the way down the hill from the campsite, her car ran out of gas, so I gave her a ride to her parents' house. We spent several more days together, hiding it from her parents because we knew it was wrong. She lied to them about going home and stayed an extra night with me. We dragged out our time together as long as we could.

"I don't want you to go," I told her. Neither one of us wanted her to leave, but she lived in Canada and said she had to go back to her husband. It was the right thing to do.

"I have to go. I don't have a choice," Mary cried.

We both cried when she left and decided we would try to see each other again soon. She started calling me after her husband went to sleep, and we'd talk in the middle of the night. Within a month, she came back for my birthday and lived in her van. She told her husband she needed a break because she wasn't happy. What he didn't know is that she was spending time with me and figuring out if she wanted to leave her husband for me.

We spent night after night in her van partying and making love. It was all fun and exciting until she found out she was pregnant. Almost instantly, we had to sober up to reality. Mary was afraid of getting caught by her husband, so she immediately scheduled an abortion. I wasn't ready to be a dad, so I didn't fight her on it. I still wanted Mary, but she was starting to have her misgivings after spending an entire month with me. I drank all the time and was selfish and arrogant. I wasn't really loving toward her, even though I was falling in love with her.

I traveled to Canada with Mary for her friend's wedding, and she planned to have the abortion while in Canada.

"In the religion I was raised in, we don't kill babies," Mary told me a few days before the abortion was supposed to take place. "I've decided not to have an abortion." She had been raised in a religious family and was taught that abortion was wrong. Even though she was having an affair with me and had never shown any remorse for what we were doing, her guilt started to mount, and the idea of her stable husband back home was looking better and better to her.

"God is tugging at my heart. I know what we're doing is wrong," Mary cried.

"Mary, God just wants us to be happy." I tried convincing her and rationalizing my perception of a loving God, despite having zero knowledge of the Bible. I didn't understand the pull she was describing. I had always believed there was a God, but I didn't know Jesus and had never had anything to do with him.

After her friend's wedding, she left without even saying goodbye. She left with my unborn baby and my heart.

∂∂∂∂

"Mary is going to take some time away from you, and you are going to give her the space she needs right now," Mary's mom, Linda, called to tell me after Mary confided in her about the baby and me.

I was confused and didn't know what to think of Mary's change of heart or the guilt she was feeling. I was curious about what in her spiritual life had forced her out of my life so quickly. I was in love with her and wanted to be with her. I didn't care if she was married, and I felt confident we could figure out how to take care of the baby. But she wouldn't even talk to me.

The longer the silence, the more curious I got about God and why her belief in him caused her remorse over what we'd done. She regretted leaving her husband and getting pregnant by another man, not to mention a man who had little more to offer than a full-time job and a full-time drinking habit.

Still curious, I opened the Bible I'd had since I was a kid.

"I'm trying to read my Bible," I told Mary's stepdad, Rob, when I called him on the phone. He wasn't very fond of me, for obvious reasons. "I started at the beginning, but it's not making any sense to me."

"If you want to start reading the Bible, start with reading the Book of John," he offered, trying to steer me in the right direction. But I still didn't understand it.

Linda arranged a meeting for me with a guy named Richard who tried to help me. We went to breakfast, then to a bookstore where I bought a new Bible written in more modern English that might help me better understand its teachings. In the front, I wrote a dedication of the Bible to "Pat," which is what I called my unborn child because I didn't know if we were having a boy or a girl. The name "Pat" worked for either gender, like the character from a recurring *Saturday Night Live* skit.

I kept my Bible in my pickup truck and read it daily. I decided that if I was ever going to have a chance of being part of my baby's life, I had better start investigating some of these things Mary was talking about and at least try to understand her. I also decided I should stop drinking, so I gave that a try, too.

చచచ

Linda gave me a book titled *Where Is God When It Hurts?* The book had really good insights that shed light on why we experience pain and how we can cope with painful experiences. Everything about the Bible, God and books like these were new to me. I was just a babe in the woods, trying to find my way to God, even if that meant trying to justify that Mary and I belonged together. More than I wanted Mary, I didn't want our baby to be born into the mess we had made. I didn't want our child to start life separated from me, so while reading the book, I decided (in my own naive way) that God was trying to tell me that he wanted Mary and me to be together. I became certain that all of this had happened because we were meant to be together. I wasn't capable of accepting that maybe God didn't want this. I didn't know God, and I didn't want to believe that being with Mary could be wrong.

During this time, I started jogging again and refrained from spending time with my partying friends. I also started praying to God, begging and bargaining with him for Mary and me to be together.

"Listen, I have been praying a lot about this," I told

Pastor Ryan, who also knew Mary and the circumstances surrounding her pregnancy. "I believe God is trying to tell me that Mary and I are *supposed* to be together."

"I assure you, son, God does *not* want you and Mary to be together. She's married to someone else," Pastor Ryan firmly told me. "You're making your relationship with God into a sham, and you should just go away and leave Mary and her family to sort this out on their own."

I was furious and decided right then and there to hate that guy.

Pastor Ryan didn't agree with me on what I thought God had told me, so I asked Mary and Linda to meet with me. I tried telling both of them about how I believed God wanted us to be together, and they, too, thought the whole idea was crazy.

Why would God allow us to meet and bring a baby into our lives if we aren't supposed to be together?

I was heartbroken. I was still bargaining with God, telling him and Mary both that I was going to change. I wanted to earn this new life that I thought God was telling me about.

❧❧❧

Shortly after I was arrested for the DUI after waving a cop over to borrow his jack, my mom's mom took me out to lunch and gave me $10,000.

"I'm confident you won't use this money to go buy a new hotrod," Nana told me. "I'm sure you can pick yourself up and put your life back together. Start focusing on doing the right things, and use this money to help get you through this."

I deposited the money and met with an attorney. He said I didn't need his help and that I needed to use the money to take the diversion program and pay my fines, so that's what I did. I lost my license for 90 days and had to rely on my dad to drive me around, much like he had relied on me when his symptoms of Parkinson's disease were at their worst. I eventually received a hardship permit so I could drive to work, but I was pretty much stuck the rest of the time. I also started alcohol counseling and began to have a better understanding of my addiction. Nana's husband owned a chain of health clubs, so I had a free membership. When I wasn't working, I exercised. I rarely drank.

My mom was in my life more and more as I got older. About the time I went to jail, she was diagnosed with breast cancer. I was so wrapped up in my own life and its drama that I couldn't really process her illness or be part of supporting her. I had spent so many years going to doctors' appointments with my dad and learning more about Parkinson's disease than I ever cared to know, and I just didn't feel prepared to learn about yet another disease, even for her sake. Even though I chose not to accompany my mom to her doctors' appointments or her chemotherapy, she showed grace and accepted my place in her life during this time, and we became closer than we had ever been. She advocated for my rights as the father of my unborn baby and hired an attorney for me in Canada after I heard through the grapevine that Mary had decided to give our baby up for adoption. Mary apparently had told her husband everything about the affair and the baby, and he evidently made it abundantly clear that if she wanted to stay married to him, there could be no baby.

"You need to just wait it out," the attorney told me. "A large percentage of the time, the mother changes her mind about adoption." Mary had moved to Alberta, Canada, which, as I understood it, was the one jurisdiction in all of Canada where if Mary wanted to put our baby up for adoption, there was nothing I could do to stop her.

Waiting proved difficult, and all of the uncertainty wore on me. I felt like there was no order in my life, no matter how hard I tried to get on the right track. For months I read my Bible, prayed and bargained with God, and kept my distance from Mary as I had been asked to do. After committing my life to Jesus, I desired a path better than the mess I had made on my own. It was no longer about wanting Mary or trying to bring us together. If I was truly seeking forgiveness for the sin of adultery with Mary, even with our baby on the way, then I also realized I had to stop wanting to be reunited with Mary. She was a married woman, so wanting her was also wrong. I realized I needed to be forgiven for simply wanting Mary. I had to let her go. While I was certain I had received this gift of forgiveness from God, I was still struggling and felt like there was so much more work for me to do.

A Guy, a Girl and a Parked Van

At that point in my relationship with Jesus, it was like I was walking down a dark flight of stairs. I was pretty sure there would be another step and another step, but the light had not come on yet to show me the way. Every time I took a step forward, it was a step of faith that Jesus would lead the way for me.

ه‍ه‍ه‍

"This is about the time women who are considering adoption often change their mind and keep the baby," my lawyer assured me when he called unexpectedly. It was March, and Mary was eight months pregnant. "But continue to leave her alone, and don't contact her."

"But I don't want her to think I'm okay with her giving the baby up for adoption," I explained.

"Trust me on this. If you start pressuring her now, it'll force her to dig in her heels and stick with her decision. It's a mental game we are playing here, but I have a good feeling it's going to work in this case," he insisted.

As hard as it was to hold back and not contact Mary, knowing our baby was just weeks away from being born, I followed my attorney's advice.

"Come down here, and visit me," my nana said. "Take some time off work, and get away for a little while. It'll take your mind off things."

My nana knew I was struggling with the waiting and paid my expenses to come to California to get my mind off things. It helped a lot. I sat by the pool and played my guitar, relaxing and spending time alone deep in prayer.

"Mary found out she is having a boy," Linda informed me when she called me in California. "She's having a boy, and she's decided to keep the baby. Someone will contact you once the baby is born."

That was it. That's all she said, but it was the best news I could have received. I was elated! And I was ready to fight for my son when he was born.

"You won't need me after all," my lawyer said when I called him with the news. "Good for you."

He kept a few hundred dollars and returned the rest of the retainer money. He was an honest guy who gave me some of the best advice of my life.

All of the promises I had been making about quitting drinking and taking more responsibility in my life suddenly had new meaning to me. The day Linda called me about the baby was when I had my last drink.

࿎࿎࿎

Life looked up for me. I still hadn't contacted Mary. I didn't want to do or say anything to change her mind. I was going to church every Sunday, had completely stopped drinking and was in great physical, mental and emotional shape. I knew I had to be ready for when my son was born.

I was jogging a lot and prayed throughout every mile. I was in constant prayer. I knew I hadn't been the loving, selfless man Mary wanted me to be when we were together, but I did believe I'd know how to be a good dad.

I knew my own loving and devoted dad had instilled the desire for fatherhood in me.

One day, when I was leaving the gym after a long workout, I was getting in my truck when my cell phone rang.

"Mary had the baby," Rob told me. "His name is Michael Andrews, and mother and baby are doing well."

It was a brief conversation, but it was all I needed to know. I had a son. I couldn't believe it. He was healthy and doing well, and Mary was keeping him. I immediately started to cry and was overwhelmed by how instantly affected I was by the news. I hadn't seen him or touched him, but I knew I was a dad, and I was grateful for him being alive and healthy. Mary had given our son her husband's last name, and I knew nothing about her situation with him, but I focused on my son and how long it would take until I could see him and hold him in my arms.

On the way home, I called everyone I knew. When I called my grandma to tell her, she didn't speak at first.

"What is it, Grandma?" I asked. I could hear her sobbing.

"Today would have been Aunt Marion's birthday."

❧❧❧

"I need you to send money for a DNA test," Mary told me. It was the first time she had initiated a conversation since months before when she'd left after her friend's wedding without saying goodbye.

"Okay, I'll send you the money." I excitedly complied with her request. "So much has happened. I went to jail for a DUI, and I've completely changed. I've stopped drinking, I've been working out and taking care of myself. I've got a good job. I also committed my life to following Jesus, Mary."

"Greg! I don't want to talk about this with you. Just send the check for the DNA test," she insisted.

"Okay, I'll send it tomorrow," I agreed. Then she hung up the phone.

The days passed slowly, and I spent them in constant prayer.

"The results are back. He's your son. What now?" Mary bluntly wrote in an email to me several days later.

"I'd like to meet him on Father's Day," I replied.

"Okay," she answered simply.

That was the most thankful moment of my life, and I was brought to my knees in tears. I felt convinced that everything I had been doing out of discipline and faith was 100 percent real. I literally felt the embrace of Jesus, and I knew that I had reached a milestone in my walk with God. Quitting drinking, taking better care of my health, focusing on working hard to support my son financially and building my relationship with God had led me to this one moment. I took a swing at something and hit the mark. I had asked Mary for a visit with my son on Father's Day, not knowing what she would say, and she said yes.

At that point, I absolutely believed God was by my side, full of mercy and compassion for me. I believed that the gift of my son had been given to me by God's grace alone, because I sure didn't feel like I deserved it. I knew Mary's and my choices resulted in a less-than-ideal way of bringing a child into the world, but I couldn't change anything that had already happened. Even though I hadn't yet figured out how Mary and I would maneuver parenthood in our circumstances, I did know what I was capable of as a dad. I had learned from my dad, and I felt like being a good father was the very best I could offer my child.

It was a lesson in letting go, because I'd had no control over what would happen since the day Mary found out she was pregnant. She could have had the abortion, given our son up for adoption or remained in Alberta and not allowed me to see him. I learned to put my faith in God alone. Thus far, the outcome had been a huge encouragement to move forward with the same type of discipline I had already been practicing. I needed to stay the course. No longer did I feel like I was walking on stairs in darkness. Instead, I felt like Jesus had lit up my life, and I was more ready than ever for whatever God had in store for me.

𝛔𝛔𝛔

"Your son will never remember if he met you on Father's Day or the day after," my boss told me when declining to give me the day off to meet Michael. I resigned on the spot. I had come too far and had too much to lose if I gave up meeting my son on Father's Day.

Exactly one year from the day I met Mary, I met my son for the first time. Holding him in my arms was like a full-circle moment for me. Everything I had been praying for was bundled up in my arms. I instantly felt the magnitude of fatherhood and knew I would do anything and everything to ensure I had an ongoing and vital place in his life.

"We need to make arrangements for child support," Mary said sharply. My first time meeting Michael was also the first time I had come face to face with Mary since she left me without saying goodbye. She wanted nothing to do with small talk.

"Well, I had to quit my job to be able to come today, but I will get something else right away and help support Michael," I told her, seeing the disappointment on her face.

She was not impressed with my being unemployed, but I had no intentions of letting my son down. Seeing Mary again, I knew that I still loved her, but it was obvious I would only be in her life as Michael's father. She wanted nothing else to do with me.

I returned home and cashed out my 401k. I used the money to pay the hospital bill from Michael's birth and immediately found a good-paying summer job. I made the decision to return to school, and my nana was so thrilled with my decision that she offered to pay me a stipend for living expenses and pay for my books and tuition.

For the next few years, I visited Michael as often as possible, went to school full time and worked enough to pay child support. Mary and I communicated often but only as it related to Michael. She never wanted to hear about how I was doing, and she didn't want me to ask her any personal questions. Our telephone conversations, in-person meetings during my visits with Michael and email exchanges were always brief and to the point.

Mary brought Michael to see me in Oregon every few months. Seeing her each time just reaffirmed my love for her. I compared every girl I met or dated to her. It was difficult, but I continued to focus on God. I also made the decision to change my major in college to math and was offered a job in the math department. I had always been good at math, and it felt like the right move.

My visits with Michael always ended too soon. I missed him horribly, and saying goodbye to him was always heartbreaking. When he was about 18 months old, Mary went on a mission trip to Guatemala and let Michael stay with me while she was gone for several days.

During our extended visit, I was reading Michael a book, as I often did, and one of the pages had a picture of a family watching a fire truck pass by.

"There's the mommy. There's the daddy. There's the son. And there's the daughter," I showed Michael as I pointed to each member of the family in the picture.

"Daddy," Michael said as he pointed at me. My heart melted. I had worried he didn't know I was his daddy because we didn't see each other every day. I still had no idea if Mary's husband was a stepdad to him or if they were even together, but when he pointed at me and called me daddy, I was assured he knew my place in his life, even if geography and circumstances kept us apart.

I had accepted the emotional distance between Mary and me, even though I was still in love with her. This was a very calm yet uncertain time in my life. I often felt like I was walking in circles. I wasn't happy, but I wasn't sad. I had no idea what God had in store for me, but I did my best to listen to him. I felt like he told me to keep walking. He didn't tell me which direction to walk, he just told me to walk.

My grandpa died just a couple months before Michael's 3rd birthday. It was a devastating loss for my family.

My father had lost his best friend, and we had all lost the head of our clan. He had adored Mary and Michael, accepting them always, no matter the circumstances.

I left for spring break at my nana's in California, which I had done each year since the first time she invited me the week Michael was born. During my visit, I called Mary on a whim.

"I'd like to come to Canada for Michael's 3rd birthday," I told Mary.

"Okay."

I was shocked. I hadn't expected her to let me come.

"I don't have enough money to get a hotel," I said.

"You can sleep in Michael's bed."

I was shocked again. I would have been happy with being offered the porch.

When I arrived at Mary's house, there was a babysitter

with Michael. I had prepared myself for Mary keeping her distance from me as she had been doing for several years. I just wanted to be with Michael and was grateful for the time with him.

When Mary got home, she and I put Michael to bed together. After we were done, I asked her to help me unload the toys from the trunk of my car that I had bought for Michael's birthday. When we got to the car, Mary playfully jumped on my back.

What is going on? I haven't seen this side of her in four years.

After we finished unloading the car, the two of us sat down to talk.

"After I left you, Justin and I were separated for almost two years. He had told me it was either him or the baby, so when I chose the baby, I figured he and I were done," Mary explained. "I spent the first two years concentrating on Michael and being a good mom. I focused on God and tried to make sense of everything that had happened. That's why I went to Guatemala for mission work. It was part of my process of finding my way back to God."

"Did you and Justin ever get back together?" I asked. I had never been able to ask Mary anything about what she was going through during the years we were apart. There was so much I wanted to know.

"He came back and said I hadn't fought for him, so we got back together and tried again. I felt like I owed him that, but I feared the damage was done and he could never accept Michael," Mary admitted. "And I was right."

"How long did it last?"

"About a year. By then, I was serious about my walk with God, and Justin still wasn't a follower of Jesus, and that made our relationship more difficult. We finally split up for good several weeks ago."

"I worried about you and wondered about you, but I tried to let you go and just concentrate on being a good dad to Michael," I told her.

"And you are a wonderful dad to him."

"I am in school full time," I told her. "I quit drinking right after your mom called to tell me we were having a boy and you weren't putting our baby up for adoption. I have been doing my best to walk with God for several years now."

"I've had feelings for you for a long time, but it's only now that I feel like I can tell you. I feel released from Justin. We have both moved on," Mary confided.

"I've never stopped loving you," I admitted, confessing my own love to her.

"When I told my family I had feelings for you, everyone said it wasn't right and started praying against it," Mary explained. "Then, it was my mom who asked everyone to start praying for my discernment. They started praying for God to bring some good from our situation."

The way we came together was not admirable by any stretch. It was complicated and difficult, and we created a miserable situation for everyone, including our son. But we believed that God had forgiven us, and we felt like this was our opportunity to get it right. We professed our love for each other and admitted we didn't want to mess it up again. By the end of the five days I spent at her house for Michael's birthday, we decided to get married. Five months later, a pastor who originally advised against our relationship saw the change that Jesus made in our lives. We weren't perfect, but we were determined to live God's way from then on. He married us surrounded by our family and friends.

❧❧❧

My dad died in 2007 due to complications related to Parkinson's disease. While it was hard to lose my best friend, I had peace about his death, largely because I believed that God was good and also because I knew my dad would no longer suffer. As a kid, I had always been afraid of my dad dying. I didn't want to go to my mom's or be gone from him for too long because I was afraid I would come back and he would be gone. He always said there would be a cure one day, but that didn't stop me from worrying about him dying before a cure could be discovered. There had always been so much fear attached to the idea of my dad's death for me. But when he finally died as an aging man who no longer wanted to suffer from his debilitating disease, I wasn't afraid anymore. I had my reasons to believe he knew God and felt he had been set free from a body that had betrayed him decades earlier.

Of the elders who helped raise Cindy and me, my

grandma was the only one still alive. My father's death was a painful and grueling loss for her, and Cindy and I did our best to get her through it until her death five years later.

❧❧❧

When Mary and I got married, my nana bought us a house. She said it was a better investment than the rent she had been paying for me since I started school. Years later, it was time for me to buy the house in my name or she would have to sell it because it was an interest-only loan, and the balloon payment was coming due.

I was at a crossroads in my education, and I was feeling the pressure to make decisions based on where I was in my life at the time. I didn't have good enough grades to get into engineering professional school, so I held back on school and briefly partnered in a local business. After our son suffered a minor injury and the medical expenses made Mary nervous, it became evident that I would need to get a job with health benefits and a more secure income.

I applied for and was offered an entry-level position working for a company that promised opportunities for advancement. I eventually rose to a position where the work was challenging, rewarding and provided health benefits and money toward retirement, which, for Mary, equaled job security. It also enabled us to buy that house from my nana.

A Guy, a Girl and a Parked Van

જ~જ~જ

Mary and I wanted to be active in church and find a church home right away when we got married. We thought it would be a good idea to start by visiting the churches closest to our home. Kings Circle was within walking distance, so we literally just walked into the church one day. It was the first church we visited and the last. Kings Circle became our church home.

The church was filled with a warm and inviting group of people. No one there cast judgment or interfered with our walk with God. We have not been met with condemnation. Even after members of our Kings Circle church family learned how we got to where we are today — many years and several kids later — we felt love for the family we created, despite the strife and suffering we caused in the beginning. God had taken something that was broken and wrong and, in his mercy, he made our lives into something beautiful.

I often thought that if Mary had left her husband after she found out she was pregnant and we had been married for the sake of our unborn son, it might not have been possible for us to have the marriage we have today. I might never have been compelled to take a look at what was bringing Mary closer to God, and I might never have found him for myself. I still would have wanted to be a good father to my son, but I don't think I would have been a good husband to his mother.

જ~જ~જ

"Come on, guys," I reasoned with our youngest child. "We're running late." Getting all of us ready and out the door for church was never a simple task. Just making sure all the kids had their shoes on the right feet was tough, but we were no different than many other families balancing a busy home with spending time worshipping God as a family.

"Where's Ella?" Mary asked.

"She wants to bring her pink Bible but can't find it," I explained.

"Ella," Mary hollered upstairs. "Two minutes. You should've looked for it last night, not when we're about to leave."

"I can grab the other kids and start walking," I suggested.

"Okay, we'll be right behind you," Mary said, then kissed me before heading upstairs to help Ella find her Bible.

As I shut the door behind us and held hands with our youngest son to cross the street and start the short walk to church, I considered the life Mary and I shared. How we began is often lost in the wonderment of our family. We haven't forgotten the lessons we learned, but we also tried not to dwell on the wrongdoing. Instead, we honored God the best we could each day, fully believing it was only through him that we could ever truly be forgiven. We believed only a perfect and good God could love us despite our past, and for that, we would be forever thankful.

Conclusion

When I became a pastor, my desire was to really help people. My hope was to see people encouraged and the hurting filled with hope. As I read this book, I saw that passion being fulfilled.

Every time we at Kings Circle Assembly see another life filled with positive results, it reminds us that God really loves people and is actively seeking to help them. Think about it: How did you get this book? We believe you received this book because God is wanting to show his love to you. Whether you're a man or a woman, a logger or a waitress, an HP employee or a professor, a parent or a university student, we believe God had you in mind. He came to redeem us from the hellish pain we've wallowed in and to offer real joy and the opportunity to share in real life that will last forever through faith in Jesus Christ.

Are you wondering if such radical change is possible? It seems too good to be true, doesn't it?

Each of us at Kings Circle Assembly invites you to come and check out our church family. Ask questions, examine our statements, see if we're "for real" and, if you choose, journey with us at whatever pace you are comfortable. You will find that we are far from perfect. Our scars and sometimes open wounds are still healing, but we just want you to know God is still completing the process of authentic life change in us. We still make mistakes on our journey, like everyone will. Because that's true, we acknowledge our continued need for each other's forgiveness and support. We need the love of God today just as much as we did the day we first believed in him.

If you are unable to hang out with us, yet you intuitively sense you would really like to experience such a life change, here are some basic thoughts to consider. If you choose, at the end of this conclusion, you can pray the suggested prayer. If your prayer genuinely comes from your heart, we believe you will experience the beginning stages of authentic life change, similar to those you have read about.

How does this change occur?

1. Recognize that what you're doing isn't working.
2. Accept the fact that Jesus desires to help you make a new start and wipe clean any record of your poor decisions or self-centered motives.
3. Realize that without this new start, you will continue a life separated from a relationship with God. In the Bible, the book of Romans, chapter 6, verse 23 tells us that the result of sin (seeking our way rather than God's way) is eternal separation from God, but the gift that God freely wants us to possess is everlasting life found in Jesus Christ.
4. Believe in your heart that God really does loves you and wants to give you a new heart. Ezekiel 11:19 reads, "I will give them singleness of heart

and put a new spirit within them. I will take away their stony, stubborn heart and give them a tender, responsive heart" (NLT).

5. Believe in your heart that "if you confess with your mouth that Jesus is Lord and believe in your heart that God raised him from the dead, you will be saved" (Romans 10:9 NLT).

6. Believe in your heart that because Jesus paid for your failure and wrong motives, and because you asked him to forgive you, he has filled your new heart with his life in such a way that he transforms you from the inside out. Second Corinthians 5:17 reads, "When someone becomes a Christian, he becomes a brand-new person inside. He is not the same anymore. A new life has begun!"

Why not pray now?

Lord Jesus, if I've learned one thing in my life's journey, it's that you are God and I am not. My choices have not resulted in the happiness I had hoped they would bring. Not only have I experienced pain, I've also caused it. I know I am separated from you, but I want that to change. I am sorry for the choices I've made that have hurt myself and others and held you at bay. I believe your death paid for my sins and that you are now alive to change me from the inside out. Would you please begin doing that now? I ask you to come and participate in my life so that I can learn to walk with you. Thank you for listening to me and beginning the change that I so desperately need. Now please help me to be aware of your guidance in my life, so I can cooperate with you in the changes you're putting in motion. Amen.

Corvallis' unfolding story of God's love is still being written — and it includes you. I hope you can come this Sunday! We meet at 10:30 a.m.

Pastor Steve Minton
Kings Circle Assembly

We would love for you to join us at Kings Circle Assembly of God!

We meet Sunday mornings at 10:30 a.m. at 2110 NW Circle Boulevard, Corvallis, OR 97330.

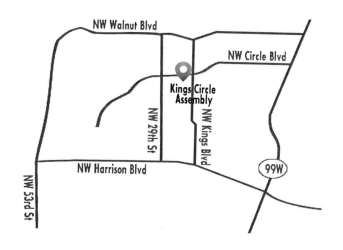

Contact Information
Phone: 541.757.9080
Web site: www.kcag.org
Email: info@kcag.org

Other Service Times
Bible Interest Groups: Sunday - 9 a.m.
Family Activity Night: Wednesday - 6:30 p.m.

For more information on reaching your city with stories from your church, go to www.testimonybooks.com.

GOOD CATCH
PUBLISHING